PENGUIN  CLASSICS

PENGUIN'S POEMS FOR LOVE

LAURA BARBER is former editorial director of Penguin Classics and now publishes contemporary literature and writes. She also selected and introduced *Penguin's Poems for Life* and *Penguin's Poems by Heart*.

Penguin's Poems *for* Love

Selected with a preface by
LAURA BARBER

PENGUIN BOOKS

PENGUIN CLASSICS

Published by the Penguin Group
Penguin Books Ltd, 80 Strand, London WC2R ORL, England
Penguin Group (USA) Inc., 375 Hudson Street, New York, New York 10014, USA
Penguin Group (Canada), 90 Eglinton Avenue East, Suite 700, Toronto, Ontario, Canada M4P 2Y3
(a division of Pearson Penguin Canada Inc.)
Penguin Ireland, 25 St Stephen's Green, Dublin 2, Ireland
(a division of Penguin Books Ltd)
Penguin Group (Australia), 250 Camberwell Road, Camberwell, Victoria 3124, Australia
(a division of Pearson Australia Group Pty Ltd)
Penguin Books India Pvt Ltd, 11 Community Centre, Panchsheel Park, New Delhi – 110 017, India
Penguin Group (NZ), 67 Apollo Drive, Rosedale, North Shore 0632, New Zealand
(a division of Pearson New Zealand Ltd)
Penguin Books (South Africa) (Pty) Ltd, 24 Sturdee Avenue, Rosebank, Johannesburg 2196, South Africa

Penguin Books Ltd, Registered Offices: 80 Strand, London WC2R ORL, England

www.penguinclassics.com

First published 2009
Published in paperback in Penguin Classics 2010
009

Selection and editorial material copyright © Laura Barber, 2009

The moral right of the editor has been asserted

The Acknowledgements on pages 349–356 constitute an extension of this copyright page

Printed in Great Britain by Clays Ltd, St Ives plc

A CIP catalogue record for this book is available from the British Library

ISBN: 978-0-140-42480-5

www.greenpenguin.co.uk

Penguin Books is committed to a sustainable
future for our business, our readers and our planet.
This book is made from Forest Stewardship
Council™ certified paper.

Contents

How do I love thee? . . .
Suddenly

Secretly

Nearly

Tentatively

Haplessly

Incurably

Impatiently

Superlatively

Persuasively

Passionately

The morning after

Greedily

Truly, madly, deeply

From a distance

With a vow

Happily ever after

Treacherously

Brutally

Bitterly

Finally

Forsaken

Regretfully

Fatally

Indifferently

After death

Eternally

How do I love thee? Let me count the ways.
I love thee to the depth and breadth and height
My soul can reach, when feeling out of sight
For the ends of Being and Ideal Grace.
I love thee to the level of everyday's
Most quiet need, by sun and candlelight.
I love thee freely, as men strive for Right;
I love thee purely, as they turn from Praise.
I love thee with a passion, put to use
In my old griefs, and with my childhood's faith.
I love thee with the love I seemed to lose
With my lost saints, – I love thee with the breath,
Smiles, tears, of all my life! – and, if God choose,
I shall but love thee better after death.

Elizabeth Barrett Browning, from
Sonnets from the Portuguese: XLIII

Preface

'I love you.' These three words, in this combination, are surely the most glorious, exhilarating and significant in the language. They're also some of the most mercurial, ambiguous and downright inadequate. 'I love you' appears to say it all, but at the same time, it doesn't even begin to cover all the things we might be feeling when we say it. There's a world of difference between the cautious 'I love you' that nudges a friendship towards romance, and the certain 'I love you' that confirms long-term commitment. And between the conciliatory 'I love you' that marks the end of domestic hostilities, and the hope-crumpling 'I love you' that's followed by a 'but . . .'. Like a magical 'abracadabra', these three words seem to contain within them almost boundless possibilities, and perhaps no one has demonstrated the sheer capaciousness of 'I love you' quite as deftly as Elizabeth Barrett Browning.

With her future husband in mind, Elizabeth Barrett Browning asked herself 'How do I love thee?' and then she started to count. In the space of just fourteen lines, she came up with at least eight different ways. And, if we look more closely at these 'ways', it quickly becomes clear that her love is straining at the seams: it extends as far as it can in all directions (depth, breadth and height) and, at the end of the poem, it bursts beyond the very limits of life itself. So, rather than offering a precise calculation of the 'ways' she loves, the poem actually proves them to be countless and immeasurable. For an accountant, this would be an infuriating situation, but luckily her lover, the poet Robert Browning, understood. On the eve of their elopement, he wrote to her:

You will only expect a few words – what will those be? When the heart is full it may run over, but the real fullness stays within . . . Words can never tell you, however, – form them, transform them anyway, – how perfectly dear you are to me – perfectly dear to my heart and soul.

Elizabeth Barrett Browning's sonnet and Robert Browning's letter seem to go to the very heart of our experience of love. When we try to say exactly *how* we love someone, it's difficult to sum it up. Our feelings can be so powerful, and so personal to us, that we struggle to put them into words. But that's where poetry can help – for if one of the conditions of being in love is feeling somewhat lost for words, then perhaps one of the conditions of being a poet in love is a belief that the right words can and *must* be found. As lovers, the Brownings were consummate word-hunters. The sonnet above was just one in a sequence of forty-four on the same theme, and during their courtship the couple exchanged hundreds of letters. They were united by a shared desire to make the language of love their own – to reshape it and re-charge it to embody the full force of their emotions. 'Say thou dost love me, love me, love me – toll the silver iterance!' she implored in another sonnet. 'Whole epics might be written,' he avowed.

Whole epics *have* been written, and odes, ballads, songs and haiku too – as poets throughout the ages have sought their own words to capture anew this most infinite and individual of emotions. This book gathers together some of the best and most beautiful of their attempts to make sense of how love feels and takes you on a journey through a few of its myriad ways.

So, where to begin? The structure of this book was inspired by Elizabeth Barrett Browning's 'How do I love thee?', so it focuses exclusively on romantic love, but the 'ways' it counts are very different. The route I have plotted takes us from the thunderbolt 'suddenly' of love at first sight to the death-defying 'eternally' of love that endures for ever, and it includes many of the familiar landmarks of the romance that finds public recognition 'with a vow' and continues along the (sometimes rocky) road of 'happily ever after'. But I also wanted to venture off in as many divergent directions as possible and to follow them through to their final destinations. I wanted to trace some of the private paths of love that we travel down, whether it be 'secretly' with an unspoken crush, 'treacherously' in an illicit passion, or 'regretfully' long after the relationship is officially over. All of these journeys are charted here, along with some more unexpected diversions, such as the 'incurably' of delirious obsession, the 'bitterly' of an affection that has coiled into acrimony, and the 'greedily' of insatiable desire. As well as traversing a varied emotional landscape, we will also roam widely through time and space, from Chaucer's love-struck knights in the fourteenth century to Isobel Dixon's irresistible ape today, and from Chinua Achebe's love letter from Nigeria to Jean 'Binta' Breeze's Jamaican 'dub' poem and Leonard Cohen's lyrics in Canada.

This inevitably makes for a somewhat tangled map, but as Shakespeare reminds us in *A Midsummer Night's Dream*, 'the course of true love never did run smooth'. This book might be best approached as you would a 'choose your own adventure' story: you can skip ahead, rest in a lay-by, go into reverse, or stop and start again at any point – much like love itself. But wherever you begin, wherever you end up, and whatever happens on the way, I hope you'll meet some interesting fellow travellers.

Given the intensely intimate nature of love, it may seem perverse to suggest that we'd want extra company. Three's generally considered to be a crowd, especially if the third person happens to be a besotted bard, a pasty-looking swain, a wise-cracking broad, or a doomed maiden intent upon watery self-destruction. And besides, who wants to think that anyone else has ever loved in the same way as we do? When we fall in love with someone, we discover things about them which strike us as uniquely adorable – and we respond in turn with what feels like unique adoration.

And yet, on either side of that heady spell of mutual rapture which transports two people to another world entirely, so many of the 'ways' of love are solitary. Think about the precarious period at the beginning of love when we're beset by silent doubts, both about how we feel and about how the other person might respond; or the feverish agonies of unrequited devotion; the icy loneliness that creeps around the bed in the middle of the night; the heart-stab shock of betrayal; or the vertiginous sorrow of loss. The very essence, the very awfulness, of these moments is that we must experience them alone. Our sense of isolation at these times may seem absolute, but the right poem lets you know that someone else, somewhere in the universe, has once felt something similar – and survived long enough to write about it. In fact, for a poet, it seems that there is almost no greater spur to creativity than a spot of romantic frustration and wretchedness. It is far easier to concentrate on finding good rhymes and exquisite metaphors without the constant distraction of kissing and gazing, and some of the finest and most moving love poems in the language have grown out of desolation. So in this book you will encounter plenty of poems that are sympathetic to your suffering: they will wallow with you, fine-tune your fury, share your grief, and indulge your most extravagant revenge fantasies. But as well as offering companionship in your misery, there will also be poems that act like any true friend, to challenge your perspective, laugh you into a better mood, and billow your spirits.

Of course, poetry is not just for the broken-hearted; it is also for the newly infatuated, the wildly happy, and the calmly glad. When it's all going well, the haziness of our emotions can be even harder to pin down in words. And we might not want to risk crushing such fragile bliss with leaden explanations. But poetry can dance where prose fears to tread. And, when lightness of touch is called for, a sensitive poem can have real and practical uses. It can serve as a discreet go-between during a tongue-tied courtship, to flatter, compliment and apply gentle pressure, with a subtlety and a steadiness we might have lost with the first glimpse. It can act as an aphrodisiac, to charm, seduce and ravish in words. It can be the icing on the cake of a wedding ceremony or a public celebration of partnership. It can spark a memory of the flames of passion and so reignite desire. And it can encapsulate an instant of pure bliss and hold it intact for eternity.

Love is a wonderful, wayward thing. It blinds us to reality, and yet it allows us to see with dazzling clarity; it plunges us to the very depths of despair, and yet it enables our hearts to soar. The poetry of love is diverse enough to encompass these contradictions and to find the beauty in love's every mood. Whether joyful or melancholy, poetry is there to remind us why we fall for love – why we willingly lose our heads for it, entangle our limbs, and bravely bare our souls. W. H. Auden defined a poet as 'a person who is passionately in love with language', and when this language is infused with love itself, it sparkles. However we feel when we come to these words, they speak straight to the heart – like 'I love you.'

A Note on the Poems

All the poems included here were either written in English or – in a few instances – have taken on a life of their own in their English translations. Beyond this, my aim has been to range as widely as possible, historically and geographically. The earliest poems in the selection were composed in the fourteenth century and the most recent are only just appearing in print; and the poets themselves come from all parts of the world, including Africa, the Caribbean, India, North America and Canada, Australia and New Zealand, Europe, the United Kingdom and the Republic of Ireland.

For ease of comprehension, older poems have been lightly modernized in punctuation and spelling, but in the few instances when modernization or standardization would completely alter the feel of the original or amount to translation (the Medieval English and dialect poems), glosses have been provided where essential and hopefully the imagination can fill in the rest. Where a definitive text has been established by editors (for example, Emily Dickinson), and for all modern works, the poems are reproduced exactly as published.

How do I love thee? . . .

Suddenly

CHRISTINA G. ROSSETTI

I wish I could remember that first day,
 First hour, first moment of your meeting me,
 If bright or dim the season, it might be
Summer or Winter for aught I can say;
So unrecorded did it slip away,
 So blind was I to see and to foresee,
 So dull to mark the budding of my tree
That would not blossom yet for many a May.
If only I could recollect it, such
 A day of days! I let it come and go
 As traceless as a thaw of bygone snow;
It seemed to mean so little, meant so much;
If only now I could recall that touch,
 First touch of hand in hand – Did one but know!

ELIZABETH JENNINGS

Light

To touch was an accord
Between life and life;
Later we said the word
And felt arrival of love
And enemies moving off.

A little apart we are,
(Still aware, still aware)
Light changes and shifts.
O slowly the light lifts
To show one star
And the darkness we were.

SIMON BARRACLOUGH

Los Alamos Mon Amour

The second before and the eternity after
the smile that split the horizon from ear to ear,
the kiss that scorched the desert dunes to glass
and sealed the sun in its frozen amber.

Eyelids are gone, along with memories
of times when the without could be withheld
from the within; when atoms kept their sanctity
and matter meant. Should I have ducked and covered?

Instead of watching oases leap into steam,
matchwood ranches blown out like flames,
and listening to livestock scream and char
in test pens on the rim of the blast.

I might have painted myself white, or built a fallout room
full of cans and bottled water but it's clear
you'd have passed between cracks, under doors,
through keyholes and down the steps to my cellar

to set me wrapping and tagging my dead.
So I must be happy your cells have been flung through mine
and your fingers are plaiting my DNA;
my chromosomes whisper *you're here to stay*.

JOHN GOWER

from *Confessio Amantis*

Pygmaleon

I finde hou whilom ther was on,
Whos name was Pymaleon,
Which was a lusti man of yowthe:
The werkes of entaile he cowthe
Above alle othre men as tho;
And thurgh fortune it fell him so,
As he whom love schal travaile,
He made an ymage of entaile
Lich to a womman in semblance
Of feture and of contienance,
So fair yit nevere was figure.
Riht as a lyves creature
Sche semeth, for of yvor whyt
He hath hire wroght of such delit,
That sche was rody on the cheke
And red on bothe hire lippes eke;
Wherof that he himself beguileth.
For with a goodly lok sche smyleth,
So that thurgh pure impression
Of his ymaginacion
With al the herte of his corage
His love upon this faire ymage
He sette, and hire of love preide;
Bot sche no word ayeinward seide.
The longe day, what thing he dede,
This ymage in the same stede

whilom once; *on* one: *entaile* sculpture; *cowthe* could (do);
as tho then; *travaile* trouble; *feture* feature; *lyves* living; *yvor* ivory;
preide prayed; *ayeinward* in answer;

6

Was evere bi, that ate mete
He wolde hire serve and preide hire ete,
And putte unto hire mowth the cuppe;
And whan the bord was taken uppe,
He hath hire into chambre nome,
And after, whan the nyht was come,
He leide hire in his bed al nakid.
He was forwept, he was forwakid,
He keste hire colde lippes ofte,
And wissheth that thei weren softe,
And ofte he rouneth in hire Ere,
And ofte his arm now hier now there
He leide, as he hir wolde embrace,
And evere among he axeth grace,
As thogh sche wiste what he mente:
And thus himself he gan tormente
Bot how it were, of his penance
He made such continuance
Fro dai to nyht, and preith so longe,
That his preiere is underfonge,
Which Venus of hire grace herde;
Be nyhte and whan that he worst ferde,
And it lay in his nakede arm,
The colde ymage he fieleth warm
Of fleissh and bon and full of lif.

---

ate mete at dinner; *nome* taken; *forwept* exhausted with weeping;
forwakid deprived of sleep; *rouneth* whispers; *wiste* knew; *underfonge* accepted;
ferde fared

SYLVIA PLATH

Love Letter

Not easy to state the change you made.
If I'm alive now, then I was dead,
Though, like a stone, unbothered by it,
Staying put according to habit.
You didn't just toe me an inch, no –
Nor leave me to set my small bald eye
Skyward again, without hope, of course,
Of apprehending blueness, or stars.

That wasn't it. I slept, say: a snake
Masked among black rocks as a black rock
In the white hiatus of winter –
Like my neighbors, taking no pleasure
In the million perfectly-chiseled
Cheeks alighting each moment to melt
My cheek of basalt. They turned to tears,
Angels weeping over dull natures,
But didn't convince me. Those tears froze.
Each dead head had a visor of ice.

And I slept on like a bent finger.
The first thing I saw was sheer air
And the locked drops rising in a dew
Limpid as spirits. Many stones lay
Dense and expressionless round about.
I didn't know what to make of it.
I shone, mica-scaled, and unfolded
To pour myself out like a fluid
Among bird feet and the stems of plants.
I wasn't fooled. I knew you at once.

8

Tree and stone glittered, without shadows.
My finger-length grew lucent as glass.
I started to bud like a March twig:
An arm and a leg, an arm, a leg.
From stone to cloud, so I ascended.
Now I resemble a sort of god
Floating through the air in my soul-shift
Pure as a pane of ice. It's a gift.

SIR ARTHUR GORGES

Her face	Her tongue	Her wit
so fair	so sweet	so sharp
first bent	then drew	then hit
mine eye	mine ear	my heart
Mine eye	Mine ear	My heart
to like	to learn	to love
her face	her tongue	her wit
doth lead	doth teach	doth move
Her face	Her tongue	Her wit
with beams	with sound	with art
doth blind	doth charm	doth knit
mine eye	mine ear	my heart
Mine eye	Mine ear	My heart
with life	with hope	with skill
her face	her tongue	her wit
doth feed	doth feast	doth fill
O face	O tongue	O wit
with frowns	with checks	with smart
wrong not	vex not	wound not
mine eye	mine ear	my heart
This eye	This ear	This heart
shall joy	shall yield	shall swear
her face	her tongue	her wit
to serve	to trust	to fear.

EMILY DICKINSON

It was a quiet way –
He asked if I was his –
I made no answer of the Tongue
But answer of the Eyes –
And then He bore me on
Before this mortal noise
With swiftness, as of Chariots
And distance, as of Wheels –
This World did drop away
As Acres from the feet
Of one that leaneth from Balloon
Opon an Ether street.
The Gulf behind was not,
The Continents were new –
Eternity it was before
Eternity was due –
No Seasons were to us –
It was not Night nor Morn –
But Sunrise stopped opon the place
And fastened it in Dawn –

JOHN MILTON

from *Paradise Lost*, Book IV

That day I oft remember, when from sleep
I first awaked, and found myself reposed
Under a shade of flow'rs, much wond'ring where
And what I was, whence thither brought, and how.
Not distant far from thence a murmuring sound
Of waters issued from a cave and spread
Into a liquid plain, then stood unmoved
Pure as th' expanse of heav'n; I thither went
With unexperienced thought, and laid me down
On the green bank, to look into the clear
Smooth lake, that to me seemed another sky.
As I bent down to look, just opposite,
A shape within the wat'ry gleam appeared
Bending to look on me: I started back,
It started back, but pleased I soon returned,
Pleased it returned as soon with answering looks
Of sympathy and love; there I had fixed
Mine eyes till now, and pined with vain desire,
Had not a voice thus warned me, What thou seest,
What there thou seest fair creature is thyself,
With thee it came and goes: but follow me,
And I will bring thee where no shadow stays
Thy coming, and thy soft embraces, he
Whose image thou art, him thou shall enjoy
Inseparably thine, to him shalt bear
Multitudes like thyself, and thence be called
Mother of human race: what could I do,
But follow straight, invisibly thus led?
Till I espied thee, fair indeed and tall,
Under a platan, yet methought less fair,
Less winning soft, less amiably mild,
Than that smooth wat'ry image; back I turned,
Thou following cried'st aloud, Return, fair Eve;

Whom fli'st thou? Whom thou fli'st, of him thou art,
His flesh, his bone; to give thee being I lent
Out of my side to thee, nearest my heart
Substantial life, to have thee by my side
Henceforth an individual solace dear;
Part of my soul I seek thee, and thee claim
My other half: with that thy gentle hand
Seized mine, I yielded.

HART CRANE

Episode of Hands

The unexpected interest made him flush.
Suddenly he seemed to forget the pain, –
Consented, – and held out
One finger from the others.

The gash was bleeding, and a shaft of sun
That glittered in and out among the wheels,
Fell lightly, warmly, down into the wound.

And as the fingers of the factory owner's son,
That knew a grip for books and tennis
As well as one for iron and leather, –
As his taut, spare fingers wound the gauze
Around the thick bed of the wound,
His own hands seemed to him
Like wings of butterflies
Flickering in sunlight over summer fields.

The knots and notches, – many in the wide
Deep hand that lay in his, – seemed beautiful.
They were like the marks of wild ponies' play, –
Bunches of new green breaking a hard turf.

And factory sounds and factory thoughts
Were banished from him by that larger, quieter hand
That lay in his with the sun upon it.
And as the bandage knot was tightened
The two men smiled into each other's eyes.

WILLIAM SHAKESPEARE

from *Antony and Cleopatra*, II, ii

ENOBARBUS:
  When she first met Mark Antony, she pursed up his heart,
    upon the river of Cydnus.
AGRIPPA:
  There she appeared indeed! Or my reporter devised well for her.
ENOBARBUS:
  I will tell you.
  The barge she sat in, like a burnished throne,
  Burned on the water. The poop was beaten gold;
  Purple the sails, and so perfumèd that
  The winds were lovesick with them. The oars were silver,
  Which to the tune of flutes kept stroke and made
  The water which they beat to follow faster,
  As amorous of their strokes. For her own person,
  It beggared all description. She did lie
  In her pavilion, cloth-of-gold of tissue,
  O'erpicturing that Venus where we see
  The fancy outwork nature. On each side her
  Stood pretty dimpled boys, like smiling cupids,
  With divers-coloured fans, whose wind did seem
  To glow the delicate cheeks which they did cool,
  And what they undid did.
AGRIPPA: O, rare for Antony!
ENOBARBUS:
  Her gentlewomen, like the Nereides,
  So many mermaids, tended her i'th' eyes,
  And made their bends adornings. At the helm
  A seeming mermaid steers. The silken tackle
  Swell with the touches of those flower-soft hands,
  That yarely frame the office. From the barge
  A strange invisible perfume hits the sense
  Of the adjacent wharfs. The city cast
  Her people out upon her; and Antony,

Enthroned i'th' market-place, did sit alone,
Whistling to th'air; which, but for vacancy,
Had gone to gaze on Cleopatra too,
And made a gap in nature.

CHRISTOPHER MARLOWE

from *Hero and Leander*, Sestiad I

And in the midst a silver altar stood;
There Hero sacrificing turtles' blood,
Veiled to the ground, veiling her eyelids close,
And modestly they opened as she rose:
Thence flew Love's arrow with the golden head,
And thus Leander was enamourèd.
Stone still he stood, and evermore he gazèd,
Till with the fire that from his count'nance blazèd
Relenting Hero's gentle heart was strook:
Such force and virtue hath an amorous look.

It lies not in our power to love or hate,
For will in us is overruled by fate.
When two are stripped, long ere the course begin
We wish that one should lose, the other win;
And one especially do we affect
Of two gold ingots like in each respect.
The reason no man knows: let it suffice,
What we behold is censured by our eyes.
Where both deliberate, the love is slight;
Who ever loved, that loved not at first sight?

He kneeled, but unto her devoutly prayed;
Chaste Hero to herself thus softly said:
'Were I the saint he worships, I would hear him,'
And as she spake those words, came somewhat near him.
He started up, she blushed as one ashamed;
Wherewith Leander much more was inflamed.
He touched her hand, in touching it she trembled:
Love deeply grounded hardly is dissembled.
These lovers parlèd by the touch of hands;
True love is mute, and oft amazèd stands.

ELIZABETH BARRETT BROWNING

from *Sonnets from the Portuguese*

XXXVIII

First time he kissed me, he but only kissed
The fingers of this hand wherewith I write;
And ever since, it grew more clean and white, . . .
Slow to world-greetings, quick with its 'Oh, list,'
When the angels speak. A ring of amethyst
I could not wear here, plainer to my sight,
Than that first kiss. The second passed in height
The first, and sought the forehead, and half missed,
Half falling on the hair. O beyond meed!
That was the chrism of love, which love's own crown
With sanctifying sweetness, did precede.
The third upon my lips was folded down
In perfect, purple state; since when, indeed,
I have been proud and said, 'My love, my own.'

With you first shown to me,
With you first known to me,
My life-time loom'd, in hope, a length of joy:
   Your voice so sweetly spoke,
   Your mind so meetly spoke,
My hopes were all of bliss without alloy,
As I, for your abode, sought out, with pride,
This house with vines o'er-ranging all its side.

   I thought of years to come,
   All free of tears to come,
When I might call you mine, and mine alone,
   With steps to fall for me,
   And day cares all for me,
And hands for ever nigh to help my own;
And then thank'd Him who had not cast my time
Too early or too late for your sweet prime.

   Then bright was dawn, o'er dew,
   And day withdrawn, o'er dew,
And mid-day glow'd on flow'rs along the ledge,
   And walls in sight, afar,
   Were shining white, afar,
And brightly shone the stream beside the sedge.
But still, the fairest light of those clear days
Seem'd that which fell along your flow'ry ways.

MAY THEILGAARD WATTS

Vision

To-day there have been lovely things
I never saw before;
Sunlight through a jar of marmalade;
A blue gate;
A rainbow
In soapsuds on dishwater;
Candlelight on butter;
The crinkled smile of a little girl
Who had new shoes with tassels;
A chickadee on a thorn-apple;
Empurpled mud under a willow,
Where white geese slept;
White ruffled curtains sifting moonlight
On the scrubbed kitchen floor;
The under side of a white-oak leaf;
Ruts in the road at sunset;
An egg yolk in a blue bowl.

My love kissed my eyes last night.

JOHN DONNE

The Good Morrow

I wonder by my troth, what thou and I
    Did till we loved? Were we not weaned till then,
But sucked on country pleasures, childishly?
    Or snorted we in the seven sleepers' den?
'Twas so; but this, all pleasures fancies be.
If ever any beauty I did see,
Which I desired, and got, 'twas but a dream of thee.

And now good morrow to our waking souls,
    Which watch not one another out of fear;
For love, all love of other sights controls,
    And makes one little room, an everywhere.
Let sea-discoverers to new worlds have gone,
Let maps to others, worlds on worlds have shown,
Let us possess one world, each hath one, and is one.

My face in thine eye, thine in mine appears,
    And true plain hearts do in the faces rest;
Where can we find two better hemispheres
    Without sharp north, without declining west?
Whatever dies was not mixed equally;
If our two loves be one, both thou and I
Love so alike, that none do slacken, none can die.

JENNY JOSEPH

The sun has burst the sky

The sun has burst the sky
Because I love you
And the river its banks.

The sea laps the great rocks
Because I love you
And takes no heed of the moon dragging it away
And saying coldly 'Constancy is not for you'.

The blackbird fills the air
Because I love you
With spring and lawns and shadows falling on lawns.

The people walk in the street and laugh
I love you
And far down the river ships sound their hooters
Crazy with joy because I love you.

Secretly

JOHN CLARE

I hid my love when young till I
Couldn't bear the buzzing of a fly;
I hid my love to my despite
Till I could not bear to look at light:
I dare not gaze upon her face
But left her memory in each place;
Where'er I saw a wild flower lie
I kissed and bade my love goodbye.

I met her in the greenest dells,
Where dewdrops pearl the wood bluebells;
The lost breeze kissed her bright blue eye,
The bee kissed and went singing by,
A sunbeam found a passage there,
A gold chain round her neck so fair;
As secret as the wild bee's song
She lay there all the summer long.

I hid my love in field and town
Till e'en the breeze would knock me down;
The bees seemed singing ballads o'er,
The fly's buzz turned a lion's roar;
And even silence found a tongue,
To haunt me all the summer long;
The riddle nature could not prove
Was nothing else but secret love.

ROBERT BROWNING

Eyes, calm beside thee (Lady, couldst thou know!)
   May turn away thick with fast gathering tears:
I glance not where all gaze: thrilling and low
    Their passionate praises reach thee – my cheek wears
    Alone no wonder when thou passest by;
    Thy tremulous lids, bent and suffused, reply
To the irrepressible homage which doth glow
    On every lip but mine: if in thine ears
Their accents linger – and thou dost recall
    Me as I stood, still, guarded, very pale,
    Beside each votarist whose lighted brow
Wore worship like an aureole, 'O'er them all
    My beauty,' thou wilt murmur, 'did prevail
Save that one only:' – Lady, couldst thou know!

WILLIAM SHAKESPEARE
from *Twelfth Night*, II, iv

VIOLA:
Say that some lady, as perhaps there is,
Hath for your love as great a pang of heart
As you have for Olivia. You cannot love her.
You tell her so. Must she not then be answered?

ORSINO:
There is no woman's sides
Can bide the beating of so strong a passion
As love doth give my heart; no woman's heart
So big to hold so much, they lack retention.
Alas, their love may be called appetite,
No motion of the liver, but the palate,
That suffer surfeit, cloyment, and revolt.
But mine is all as hungry as the sea,
And can digest as much. Make no compare
Between that love a woman can bear me
And that I owe Olivia.

VIOLA: Ay, but I know –

ORSINO:
What dost thou know?

VIOLA:
Too well what love women to men may owe.
In faith, they are as true of heart as we.
My father had a daughter loved a man –
As it might be perhaps, were I a woman,
I should your lordship.

ORSINO: And what's her history?

VIOLA:
A blank, my lord. She never told her love,
But let concealment, like a worm i'the bud,
Feed on her damask cheek. She pined in thought,
And with a green and yellow melancholy,
She sat like Patience on a monument,

Smiling at grief. Was not this love indeed?
We men may say more, swear more, but indeed
Our shows are more than will; for still we prove
Much in our vows, but little in our love.

ORSINO:
But died thy sister of her love, my boy?

VIOLA:
I am all the daughters of my father's house,
And all the brothers too; and yet, I know not . . .
Sir, shall I to this lady?

ORSINO: Ay, that's the theme.
To her in haste; give her this jewel; say
My love can give no place, bide no denay.

CAROL ANN DUFFY
Warming Her Pearls

Next to my own skin, her pearls. My mistress
bids me wear them, warm them, until evening
when I'll brush her hair. At six, I place them
round her cool white throat. All day I think of her,

resting in the Yellow Room, contemplating silk
or taffeta, which gown tonight? She fans herself
whilst I work willingly, my slow heat entering
each pearl. Slack on my neck, her rope.

She's beautiful. I dream about her
in my attic bed; picture her dancing
with tall men, puzzled by my faint, persistent scent
beneath her French perfume, her milky stones.

I dust her shoulders with a rabbit's foot,
watch the soft blush seep through her skin
like an indolent sigh. In her looking glass
my red lips part as though I want to speak.

Full moon. Her carriage brings her home. I see
her every movement in my head . . . Undressing,
taking off her jewels, her slim hand reaching
for the case. Slipping naked into bed, the way

she always does . . . And I lie here awake,
knowing the pearls are cooling even now
in the room where my mistress sleeps. All night
I feel their absence and I burn.

WILLIAM BLAKE

The Sick Rose

O Rose thou art sick.
The invisible worm,
That flies in the night
In the howling storm:

Has found out thy bed
Of crimson joy:
And his dark secret love
Does thy life destroy.

WALLACE STEVENS

Gray Room

Although you sit in a room that is gray,
Except for the silver
Of the straw-paper,
And pick
At your pale white gown;
Or lift one of the green beads
Of your necklace,
To let it fall;
Or gaze at your green fan
Printed with the red branches of a red willow;
Or, with one finger,
Move the leaf in the bowl –
The leaf that has fallen from the branches of the
    forsythia
Beside you . . .
What is all this?
I know how furiously your heart is beating.

WILFRED OWEN

Maundy Thursday

Between the brown hands of a server-lad
The silver cross was offered to be kissed.
The men came up, lugubrious, but not sad,
And knelt reluctantly, half-prejudiced.
(And kissing, kissed the emblem of a creed.)
Then mourning women knelt; meek mouths they had,
(And kissed the Body of the Christ indeed.)
Young children came, with eager lips and glad.
(These kissed a silver doll, immensely bright.)
Then I, too, knelt before that acolyte.
Above the crucifix I bent my head:
The Christ was thin, and cold, and very dead:
And yet I bowed, yea, kissed – my lips did cling.
(I kissed the warm live hand that held the thing.)

SARAH FYGE EGERTON

A Song

How pleasant is love
When forbid or unknown;
Was my passion approved,
It would quickly be gone.

It adds to the charms
When we steal the delight;
Why should love be exposed
Since himself has no sight?

In some sylvan shade
Let me sigh for my swain,
Where none but an echo
Will speak on't again.

Thus silent and soft
I'll pass the time on,
And when I grow weary
I'll make my love known.

Nearly

JEAN 'BINTA' BREEZE

Dubwise

'cool an
    deadly'
snake
    lady
writhing
    'roun
de worlie'
  wraps
   her sinews
roun his
  pulse
  and grinds
  his pleasure
  and disgust
   into a
    one dance
  stand

to equalise
  he grins
    cockwise
   at his bredrin
  and rides
   a 'horseman scabie'
  or bubbles a
   'water
    bumpie'
  into action

             the d.j.
                 eases a
                 spliff
                 from his lyrical
                 lips
                 and smilingly
                     orders
                     'Cease'

JOHN DRYDEN

Song: from *An Evening's Love*

Calm was the Even, and clear was the sky
  And the new budding flowers did spring,
When all alone went Amyntas and I
  To hear the sweet Nightingale sing;
I sat, and he laid him down by me;
  But scarcely his breath he could draw;
For when with a fear he began to draw near,
  He was dash'd with A ha ha ha ha!

He blush'd to himself, and lay still for a while,
  And his modesty curb'd his desire;
But straight I convinc'd all his fear with a smile,
  Which added new flames to his fire.
'O Sylvia', he said, 'you are cruel,
  To keep your poor Lover in awe';
Then once more he pressed with his hand to my breast,
But was dash'd with A ha ha ha ha!

I knew 'twas his passion that caus'd all his fear;
  And therefore I pitied his case:
I whisper'd him softly 'There's no body near',
  And laid my cheek close to his face:
But as he grew bolder and bolder,
  A Shepherd came by us and saw;
And just as our bliss we began with a kiss,
  He laughed out with A ha ha ha ha!

THOMAS HARDY

A Thunderstorm in Town

She wore a new 'terra-cotta' dress,
And we stayed, because of the pelting storm,
Within the hansom's dry recess,
Though the horse had stopped; yea, motionless
    We sat on, snug and warm.

Then the downpour ceased, to my sharp sad pain,
And the glass that had screened our forms before
Flew up, and out she sprang to her door:
I should have kissed her if the rain
    Had lasted a minute more.

CONNIE BENSLEY

A Friendship

He made restless forays
into the edge of our marriage.
One Christmas Eve he came late,
his dark hair crackling with frost,
and ate his carnation buttonhole
to amuse the baby.

When I had a second child
he came to the foot of my bed at dusk
bringing pineapples and champagne,
whispering 'Are you awake?' –
singing a snatch of opera.
The Nurse tapped him on the shoulder.

At the end, we took turns at his bedside.
I curled up in the chair; listened to each breath
postponing itself indefinitely.
He opened his eyes once and I leaned forward:
'Is there anything you want?'
'Now she asks,' he murmured.

Tentatively

ARTHUR HUGH CLOUGH

from *Amours de Voyage*, Canto II

X Claude to Eustace

I am in love, meantime, you think; no doubt you would think so.
I am in love, you say; with those letters, of course, you would say
    so.
I am in love, you declare. I think not so; yet I grant you
It is a pleasure, indeed, to converse with this girl. Oh, rare gift,
Rare felicity, this! she can talk in a rational way, can
Speak upon subjects that really are matters of mind and of
    thinking,
Yet in perfection retain her simplicity; never, one moment,
Never, however you urge it, however you tempt her, consents to
Step from ideas and fancies and loving sensations to those vain
Conscious understandings that vex the minds of man-kind.
No, though she talk, it is music; her fingers desert not the keys;
    'tis
Song, though you hear in the song the articulate vocables
    sounded,
Syllabled singly and sweetly the words of melodious meaning.
  I am in love, you say; I do not think so exactly.

CAROLINE ELIZABETH
SARAH NORTON

I do not love thee! – no! I do not love thee!
And yet when thou art absent I am sad;
    And envy even the bright blue sky above thee,
Whose quiet stars may see thee and be glad.

I do not love thee! – yet, I know not why,
Whate'er thou dost seems still well done, to me:
    And often in my solitude I sigh
That those I do love are not more like thee!

I do not love thee! – yet, when thou art gone,
I hate the sound (though those who speak be dear)
    Which breaks the lingering echo of the tone
Thy voice of music leaves upon my ear.

I do not love thee! – yet thy speaking eyes,
With their deep, bright, and most expressive blue,
    Between me and the midnight heaven arise,
Oftener than any eyes I ever knew.

I know I do not love thee! yet, alas!
Others will scarcely trust my candid heart;
    And oft I catch them smiling as they pass,
Because they see me gazing where thou art.

BRIAN PATTEN

Forgetmeknot

She loves him, she loves him not, she is confused:
She picks a fist of soaking grass and fingers it:
She loves him not.
The message passing from her head to heart
Has in her stomach stopped,
She cannot quite believe the information is correct:
She loves him not.
She knows her needs and yet
There is no special place where they can rest.
To be loved alone is not enough,
She feels something has been lost.
She picks a fist of soaking grass.
Her world is blank, she thinks perhaps it's
        meaningless.

SIR PHILIP SIDNEY

from *Astrophil and Stella*

I

Loving in truth, and fain in verse my love to show,
That she (dear she) might take some pleasure of my pain;
Pleasure might cause her read, reading might make her know;
Knowledge might pity win, and pity grace obtain;
   I sought fit words to paint the blackest face of woe,
Studying inventions fine, her wits to entertain;
Oft turning others' leaves, to see if thence would flow
Some fresh and fruitful showers upon my sun-burned brain.
   But words came halting forth, wanting invention's stay;
Invention, nature's child, fled step-dame study's blows;
And others' feet still seemed but strangers in my way.
Thus, great with child to speak, and helpless in my throes,
   Biting my truant pen, beating myself for spite,
   'Fool,' said my muse to me; 'look in thy heart and write.'

BERNARD O'DONOGHUE

Stealing Up

I've always hated gardening: the way
The earth gets under your nails
And in the chevrons of your shoes.
So I don't plan it; I steal up on it,
Casually, until I find –
Hey presto! – the whole lawn's cut
Or the sycamore's wand suddenly
Sports an ungainly, foal-like leaf.

Similarly, I'd have written to you
Sooner, if I'd had the choice.
But morning after morning I woke up
To find the same clouds in the sky,
Disabling the heart. But tomorrow
Maybe I'll get up to find an envelope,
Sealed, addressed to you, propped against
My cup, lit by a slanting sun.

WILLIAM SHAKESPEARE

from *Romeo and Juliet*, II, ii

ROMEO:

But soft! what light through yonder window breaks?
It is the east and Juliet is the sun!
Arise fair sun and kill the envious moon
Who is already sick and pale with grief
That thou her maid art far more fair than she.
Be not her maid since she is envious,
Her vestal livery is but sick and green
And none but fools do wear it. Cast it off.
It is my lady, O it is my love!
O that she knew she were!
She speaks, yet she says nothing. What of that?
Her eye discourses, I will answer it.
I am too bold. 'Tis not to me she speaks.
Two of the fairest stars in all the heaven,
Having some business, do entreat her eyes
To twinkle in their spheres till they return.
What if her eyes were there, they in her head?
The brightness of her cheek would shame those stars
As daylight doth a lamp. Her eyes in heaven
Would through the airy region stream so bright
That birds would sing and think it were not night.
See how she leans her cheek upon her hand.
O that I were a glove upon that hand,
That I might touch that cheek.

JULIET:

Ay me.

ROMEO:

She speaks.
O speak again bright angel, for thou art
As glorious to this night, being o'er my head,
As is a winged messenger of heaven
Unto the white-upturned wondering eyes

Of mortals that fall back to gaze on him
When he bestrides the lazy-puffing clouds
And sails upon the bosom of the air.

JULIET:
O Romeo, Romeo, wherefore art thou Romeo?
Deny thy father and refuse thy name.
Or if thou wilt not, be but sworn my love
And I'll no longer be a Capulet.

ROMEO:
Shall I hear more, or shall I speak at this?

THOM GUNN

Jamesian

Their relationship consisted
In discussing if it existed.

JACOB SAM-LA ROSE

Things That Could Happen

1.
She swoons, falls into his arms
and they live together happily ever after.

2.
She kisses him: the restaurant applauds.

3.
There's a pin-drop silence. She turns
the knife in her hand, slowly.

4.
His heart bursts in his mouth before he can say the words.
It splatters the table, ruins her dress, and she never forgives
    him.

5.
He's interrupted by a handsome man from another table
who asks if he can cut in. She accepts, of course,
and waltzes off to an orchestra of cutlery, side-plates,
strummed napkins and warm bread. He seethes, turns bald
and tells the story to every man he meets.

6.
She falls in love with the waiter.

7.
She falls in love with the waitress.

8.
She starts by saying that she's quitting the country,
that there's nothing in London to keep her.

9.
He loses his voice, has to write it all down.
She spills a glass of wine, the ink blurs and swims
across the page. *I'm sorry* she says, and he nods,
his eyes turning to crystal.

10.
They laugh.

11.
They have passionate sex in the single toilet.
Outside, a lengthening queue tuts and frets.
Someone presses their ear to the door.

12.
She doesn't believe him.

13.
They have 3 children. Some nights, she tells them
(again) how their father won her heart
over chicken gyoza and ebi katsu.
Whenever he hears this, something in him rises
like a bull-chested spinnaker.

14.
Her mobile rings. The moment falls, like a crumb,
to the napkin in her lap. She brushes it away.

15.
He learns a new language – says it in French or Swahili.
She's mightily impressed, but doesn't understand.

16.
She chokes on a noodle. The tips of her fingers turn blue
as she fights for breath, and fails. Later, he learns to love
the bite of alcohol and numbs his tongue with ice.

17.
She chokes on a noodle. He Heimlichs her.
She sees him in a different light,
as he dabs the sparkling sputum
from her lips.

18.
He watches the way she eats
and thinks better of saying anything.

19.
Before he can speak, she leans across the table,
fingers barely touching the corners of his mouth,
and says *I know, already. I know.*

GEORGE HERBERT

Love

Love bade me welcome: yet my soul drew back,
    Guilty of dust and sin.
But quick-eyed Love, observing me grow slack
    From my first entrance in,
Drew nearer to me, sweetly questioning,
    If I lacked any thing?

'A guest', I answered, 'worthy to be here':
    Love said, 'You shall be he.'
'I the unkind, ungrateful? Ah my dear,
    I cannot look on thee.'
Love took my hand, and smiling did reply,
    'Who made the eyes but I?'

'Truth, Lord, but I have marred them: let my shame
    Go where it doth deserve.'
'And know you not', says Love, 'who bore the blame?'
    'My dear, then I will serve.'
'You must sit down', says Love, 'and taste my meat':
    So I did sit and eat.

OLIVIA MCCANNON

Timing

It's now my love for you is perfect as an egg
Soft-boiled – a quail's egg with a mottled shell
Whose markings are the landscape of our world.

I peel – the skin is soft between my teeth
I roll it on my tongue and taste its heat
Then I choose to bite and eat or keep it whole.

WALT WHITMAN

Are You the New Person Drawn toward Me?

Are you the new person drawn toward me?
To begin with take warning, I am surely far different from what
 you suppose;
Do you suppose you will find in me your ideal?
Do you think it so easy to have me become your lover?
Do you think the friendship of me would be unalloy'd
 satisfaction?
Do you think I am trusty and faithful?
Do you see no further than this façade, this smooth and tolerant
 manner of me?
Do you suppose yourself advancing on real ground toward a real
 heroic man?
Have you no thought O dreamer that it may be all maya,
 illusion?

W. B. YEATS

He Wishes for the Cloths of Heaven

Had I the heavens' embroidered cloths,
Enwrought with golden and silver light,
The blue and the dim and the dark cloths
Of night and light and the half-light,
I would spread the cloths under your feet:
But I, being poor, have only my dreams;
I have spread my dreams under your feet;
Tread softly because you tread on my dreams.

ALICE OSWALD

Sonnet

I can't sleep in case a few things you said
no longer apply. The matter's endless,
but definitions alter what's ahead
and you and words are like a hare and tortoise.
Aaaagh there's no description – each a fractal
sectioned by silences, we have our own
skins to feel through and fall back through – awful
to make so much of something so unknown.
But even I – some shower-swift commitments
are all you'll get; I mustn't gauge or give
more than I take – which is a way to balance
between misprision and belief in love
both true and false, because I'm only just
short of a word to be the first to trust.

GALWAY KINNELL

Kissing the Toad

Somewhere this dusk
a girl puckers her mouth
and considers kissing
the toad a boy has plucked
from the cornfield and hands
her with both hands,
rough and lichenous
but for the immense ivory belly,
like those old fat cats
sprawling on Mediterranean beaches,
with popped eyes,
it watches the girl who might kiss it,
pisses, quakes, tries
to make its smile wider:
to love on, oh yes, to love on.

Haplessly

AMY LOWELL

The Bungler

You glow in my heart
Like the flames of uncounted candles.
But when I go to warm my hands,
My clumsiness overturns the light,
And then I stumble
Against the tables and chairs.

EDMUND SPENSER

from *Amoretti*

XXX

My love is like to ice, and I to fire:
    how comes it then that this her cold so great
    is not dissolv'd through my so hot desire,
    but harder grows the more I her entreat?
Or how comes it that my exceeding heat
    is not delayed by her heart frozen cold,
    but that I burn much more in boiling sweat,
    and feel my flames augmented manifold?
What more miraculous thing may be told
    that fire, which all things melt, should harden ice;
    and ice, which is congealed with senseless cold,
    should kindle fire by wonderful device?
Such is the power of love in gentle mind
    that it can alter all the course of kind.

W. B. YEATS

The Song of Wandering Aengus

I went out to the hazel wood,
Because a fire was in my head,
And cut and peeled a hazel wand,
And hooked a berry to a thread;
And when white moths were on the wing,
And moth-like stars were flickering out,
I dropped the berry in a stream
And caught a little silver trout.

When I had laid it on the floor
I went to blow the fire aflame,
But something rustled on the floor,
And some one called me by my name;
It had become a glimmering girl
With apple blossom in her hair
Who called me by my name and ran
And faded through the brightening air.

Though I am old with wandering
Through hollow lands and hilly lands,
I will find out where she has gone,
And kiss her lips and take her hands;
And walk among long dappled grass,
And pluck till time and times are done
The silver apples of the moon,
The golden apples of the sun.

Thrice toss these oaken ashes in the air,
Thrice sit thou mute in this enchanted chair;
Then thrice three times tie up this true love's knot.
And murmur soft: 'She will, or she will not.'

Go burn these poisonous weeds in yon blue fire,
These screech-owl's feathers and this prickling briar,
This cypress gathered at a dead man's grave,
That all thy fears and cares an end may have.

Then come, you fairies, dance with me a round;
Melt her hard heart with your melodious sound.
In vain are all the charms I can devise;
She hath an art to break them with her eyes.

THOMAS HARDY

A Broken Appointment

You did not come,
And marching Time drew on, and wore me numb. –
Yet less for loss of your dear presence there
Than that I thus found lacking in your make
That high compassion which can overbear
Reluctance for pure lovingkindness' sake
Grieved I, when, as the hope-hour stroked its sum,
You did not come.

You love not me,
And love alone can lend you loyalty;
– I know and knew it. But, unto the store
Of human deeds divine in all but name,
Was it not worth a little hour or more
To add yet this: Once you, a woman, came
To soothe a time-torn man; even though it be
You love not me?

JOHN CROWE RANSOM

Piazza Piece

– I am a gentleman in a dustcoat trying
To make you hear. Your ears are soft and small
And listen to an old man not at all,
They want the young men's whispering and sighing.
But see the roses on your trellis dying
And hear the spectral singing of the moon;
For I must have my lovely lady soon,
I am a gentleman in a dustcoat trying.

– I am a lady young in beauty waiting
Until my truelove comes, and then we kiss.
But what grey man among the vines is this
Whose words are dry and faint as in a dream?
Back from my trellis, Sir, before I scream!
I am a lady young in beauty waiting.

STEVIE SMITH

Infelice

Walking swiftly with a dreadful duchess,
He smiled too briefly, his face was as pale as sand,
He jumped into a taxi when he saw me coming,
Leaving me alone with a private meaning,
He loves me so much, my heart is singing.
Later at the Club when I rang him in the evening
They said: Sir Rat is dining, is dining, is dining,
No Madam, he left no message, ah how his silence speaks,
He loves me too much for words, my heart is singing.
The Pullman seats are here, the tickets for Paris, I am waiting,
Presently the telephone rings, it is his valet speaking,
Sir Rat is called away, to Scotland, his constituents,
(Ah the dreadful duchess, but he loves me best)
Best pleasure to the last, my heart is singing.
One night he came, it was four in the morning,
Walking slowly upstairs, he stands beside my bed,
Dear darling, lie beside me, it is too cold to stand speaking,
He lies down beside me, his face is like the sand,
He is in a sleep of love, my heart is singing.
Sleeping softly softly, in the morning I must wake him,
And waking he murmurs, I only came to sleep.
The words are so sweetly cruel, how deeply he loves me,
I say them to myself alone, my heart is singing.
Now the sunshine strengthens, it is ten in the morning,
He is so timid in love, he only needs to know,
He is my little child, how can he come if I do not call him,
I will write and tell him everything, I take the pen and write:
I love you so much, my heart is singing.

EPHELIA

To One That Asked Me Why I Loved J.G.

Why do I love? go ask the glorious sun
Why every day it round the world doth run:
Ask Thames and Tiber why they ebb and flow:
Ask damask roses why in June they blow:
Ask ice and hail the reason why they're cold:
Decaying beauties, why they will grow old:
They'll tell thee, Fate, that everything doth move,
Inforces them to this, and me to love.
There is no reason for our love or hate,
'Tis irresistible as Death or Fate;
'Tis not his face; I've sense enough to see,
That is not good, though doated on by me:
Nor is't his tongue, that has this conquest won,
For that at least is equalled by my own:
His carriage can to none obliging be,
'Tis rude, affected, full of vanity:
Strangely ill natur'd, peevish and unkind,
Unconstant, false, to jealousy inclin'd:
His temper could not have so great a power,
'Tis mutable, and changes every hour:
Those vigorous years that women so adore
Are past in him: he's twice my age and more;
And yet I love this false, this worthless man,
With all the passion that a woman can;
Doat on his imperfections, though I spy
Nothing to love; I love, and know not why.
Since 'tis decreed in the dark book of Fate,
That I should love, and he should be ingrate.

62

SIR JOHN SUCKLING

Against Fruition

Fie upon hearts that burn with mutual fire;
I hate two minds that breathe but one desire;
Were I to curse th' unhallowed sort of men,
I'd wish them to love, and be loved again.
Love's a chameleon that lives on mere air,
And surfeits when it comes to grosser fare:
'Tis petty jealousies and little fears,
Hopes joined with doubts, and joys with April tears,
That crowns our love with pleasures: these are gone
When once we come to full fruition;
Like waking in a morning, when all night
Our fancy hath been fed with true delight.
Oh! what a stroke 't would be! Sure I should die
Should I but hear my mistress once say 'ay'.
That monster Expectation feeds too high
For any woman e'er to satisfy:
And no brave spirit ever cared for that
Which in down-beds with ease he could come at.
She's but an honest whore that yields, although
She be as cold as ice, as pure as snow:
He that enjoys her hath no more to say
But 'Keep us fasting if you'll have us pray.'
Then, fairest mistress, hold the power you have
By still denying what we still do crave:
In keeping us in hopes strange things to see
That never were, nor are, nor e'er shall be.

ROBERT BROWNING

Life in a Love

Escape me?
Never –
Beloved!
While I am I, and you are you,
    So long as the world contains us both,
    Me the loving and you the loth,
While the one eludes, must the other pursue.
My life is a fault at last, I fear:
    It seems too much like a fate, indeed!
    Though I do my best I shall scarce succeed.
But what if I fail of my purpose here?
It is but to keep the nerves at strain,
    To dry one's eyes and laugh at a fall,
And, baffled, get up and begin again, –
    So the chase takes up one's life, that's all.
While, look but once from your farthest bound
    At me so deep in the dust and dark,
No sooner the old hope goes to ground
    Than a new one, straight to the self-same mark,
I shape me –
Ever
Removed!

Incurably

DOROTHY PARKER

Symptom Recital

I do not like my state of mind;
I'm bitter, querulous, unkind.
I hate my legs, I hate my hands,
I do not yearn for lovelier lands.
I dread the dawn's recurrent light;
I hate to go to bed at night.
I snoot at simple, earnest folk.
I cannot take the gentlest joke.
I find no peace in paint or type.
My world is but a lot of tripe.
I'm disillusioned, empty-breasted.
For what I think, I'd be arrested.
I am not sick, I am not well.
My quondam dreams are shot to hell.
My soul is crushed, my spirit sore;
I do not like me any more.
I cavil, quarrel, grumble, grouse.
I ponder on the narrow house.
I shudder at the thought of men . . .
I'm due to fall in love again.

Love is a sickness full of woes,
All remedies refusing;
A plant that with most cutting grows,
Most barren with best using.
                    Why so?
More we enjoy it, more it dies;
If not enjoyed, it sighing cries,
                    Hey ho.
Love is a torment of the mind,
A tempest everlasting;
And Jove hath made it of a kind,
Not well, nor full nor fasting.
                    Why so?
More we enjoy it, more it dies;
If not enjoyed, it sighing cries,
                    Hey ho.

Dunt Dunt Dunt Pittie Pattie

On Whitsunday morning
I went to the fair
my yellowhaird laddie
was selling his ware
he gied me sic a blythe blink
with his bonny black ee
and a dear blink and a fair blink
it was unto me

I wist not what ailed me
when my laddie cam in
the little wee sternies
flew aye frae my een
and the sweat it dropped down
from my very ee bree
for my heart aye played
dunt dunt dunt pittie pattie

I wist not what ailed me
when I went to my bed
I tossd and I tumbled
and sleep frae me fled
now its sleeping and waking
he's aye in my ee
and my heart aye plays
dunt dunt dunt pittie pattie

JOHN KEATS

La Belle Dame sans Merci. A Ballad

O what can ail thee, knight-at-arms,
    Alone and palely loitering?
The sedge has withered from the lake,
    And no birds sing.

O what can ail thee, knight-at-arms,
    So haggard and so woe-begone?
The squirrel's granary is full,
    And the harvest's done.

I see a lily on thy brow,
    With anguish moist and fever-dew,
And on thy cheeks a fading rose
    Fast withereth too.

I met a lady in the meads,
    Full beautiful – a faery's child,
Her hair was long, her foot was light,
    And her eyes were wild.

I made a garland for her head,
    And bracelets too, and fragrant zone;
She looked at me as she did love,
    And made sweet moan.

I set her on my pacing steed,
    And nothing else saw all day long,
For sidelong would she bend, and sing
    A faery's song.

She found me roots of relish sweet,
    And honey wild, and manna-dew,
And sure in language strange she said –
    'I love thee true'.

She took me to her elfin grot,
    And there she wept and sighed full sore,
And there I shut her wild wild eyes
    With kisses four.

And there she lullèd me asleep
    And there I dreamed – Ah! woe betide! –
The latest dream I ever dreamt
    On the cold hill side.

I saw pale kings and princes too,
    Pale warriors, death-pale were they all;
They cried – 'La Belle Dame sans Merci
    Thee hath in thrall!'

I saw their starved lips in the gloam,
    With horrid warning gapèd wide,
And I awoke and found me here,
    On the cold hill's side.

And this is why I sojourn here
    Alone and palely loitering,
Though the sedge is withered from the lake,
    And no birds sing.

Alas, so all things now do hold their peace,
Heaven and earth disturbed in nothing.
The beasts, the air, the birds their song do cease,
The night's chair the stars about doth bring.
Calm is the sea, the waves work less and less:
So am not I, whom love, alas, doth wring,
Bringing before my face the great increase
Of my desires, whereat I weep and sing
In joy and woe as in a doubtful ease.
For my sweet thoughts sometime do pleasure bring,
But by and by the cause of my disease
Gives me a pang that inwardly doth sting,
When that I think what grief it is again
To live and lack the thing should rid my pain.

WILLIAM SHAKESPEARE

Sonnet 147

My love is as a fever, longing still
For that which longer nurseth the disease;
Feeding on that which doth preserve the ill,
The uncertain sickly appetite to please.
My reason, the physician to my love,
Angry that his prescriptions are not kept,
Hath left me, and I desperate now approve
Desire is death, which physic did except.
Past cure I am, now reason is past care.
And frantic-mad with evermore unrest;
My thoughts and my discourse as madmen's are,
At random from the truth vainly express'd;
   For I have sworn thee fair, and thought thee bright,
   Who art as black as hell, as dark as night.

D. H. LAWRENCE

Bei Hennef

The little river twittering in the twilight,
The wan, wondering look of the pale sky,
　This is almost bliss.

And everything shut up and gone to sleep,
All the troubles and anxieties and pain
　Gone under the twilight.

Only the twilight now, and the soft 'Sh!' of the river
　That will last for ever.

And at last I know my love for you is here;
I can see it all, it is whole like the twilight,
It is large, so large, I could not see it before,
Because of the little lights and flickers and interruptions,
　Troubles, anxieties and pains.

　　You are the call and I am the answer,
　　You are the wish, and I the fulfilment,
　　You are the night, and I the day.
　　　What else? it is perfect enough.
　　　It is perfectly complete,
　　　You and I,
　　　What more –?

Strange, how we suffer in spite of this!

EMILY GROSHOLZ

On Spadina Avenue

Driven by love and curiosity,
I entered the painted shops along Toronto's
Chinatown, and lingered
in one red pharmacy, where every label
was printed in mysterious characters.
Beside myself, not knowing what I stopped for,
I read the scrolling dragons, roots, and flowers
intelligible as nature,
and quizzed the apothecary on her products.

Lovesick for my husband. She was puzzled,
for how could I explain
my private fevers to a perfect stranger?
I questioned her obliquely, hit-or-miss:
Lady, what's this button full of powder?
What's this ointment in the scaly tube?
Who are these dry creatures in the basket
and how are they applied?
The deer tails gleamed in fat, uneven rows,
unrolled sea horses darkened on the shelves,
and other customers with clearer motives
stepped in behind my back.

I couldn't say, his troublesome male beauty
assails me sometimes, watching him at night
next to the closet door
half-dressed, or naked on the bed beside me.
An evening amorousness keeps me awake
for hours brooding, even after love:
how fast in time we are,
how possibly my love could quit this world
and pull down half of heaven when he goes.

The patient Chinese lady has no cure,
and serves her other customers in order.
Across the curled-up, quiet, ochre lizards,
giant starfish, quince, and ginger root,
she turns to look at me.
We both know I'm not ill with this or that,
but suffer from a permanent condition,
a murmur of the heart, the heart itself
calling me out of dreams
to verify my warm, recurrent husband
who turns and takes me in his arms again
and sleepily resumes his half of heaven.

ELIZABETH THOMAS
Remedia Amoris

Love, and the *Gout* invade the idle *Brain*,
Busyness prevents the *Passion*, and the *Pain*:
Ceres, and *Bacchus*, envious of our *Ease*,
Blow up the *Flame*, and heighten the *Disease*.
Withdraw the *Fuel*, and the *Fire* goes out;
Hard Beds, and *Fasting*, cure both *Love* and *Gout*.

WALTER SAVAGE LANDOR
Hearts-Ease

There is a flower I wish to wear,
　But not until first worn by you.
Hearts-ease: of all Earth's flowers most rare;
　Bring it; and bring enough for two.

Impatiently

Song

Go, lovely rose,
Tell her that wastes her time and me,
　That now she knows
When I resemble her to thee
　How sweet and fair she seems to be.

　Tell her that's young,
And shuns to have her graces spied,
　That hadst thou sprung
In deserts where no men abide,
　Thou must have uncommended died.

　Small is the worth
Of beauty from the light retired;
　Bid her come forth,
Suffer herself to be desired,
　And not blush so to be admired.

　Then die that she
The common fate of all things rare
　May read in thee;
How small a part of time they share
　That are so wondrous sweet and fair.

EMILY DICKINSON

If you were coming in the Fall,
I'd brush the Summer by
With half a smile, and half a spurn,
As Housewives do, a Fly.

If I could see you in a year,
I'd wind the months in balls –
And put them each in separate Drawers,
For fear the numbers fuse –

If only Centuries, delayed,
I'd count them on my Hand,
Subtracting, till my fingers dropped
Into Van Dieman's Land.

If certain, when this life was out –
That yours and mine, should be –
I'd toss it yonder, like a Rind,
And take Eternity –

But, now, uncertain of the length
Of this, that is between,
It goads me, like the Goblin Bee –
That will not state – its sting.

ALFRED, LORD TENNYSON

Mariana

'Mariana in the moated grange'
Measure for Measure

With blackest moss the flower-plots
    Were thickly crusted, one and all:
The rusted nails fell from the knots
    That held the pear to the gable-wall.
The broken sheds look'd sad and strange:
    Unlifted was the clinking latch;
    Weeded and worn the ancient thatch
Upon the lonely moated grange.
        She only said, 'My life is dreary,
            He cometh not,' she said;
        She said, 'I am aweary, aweary,
            I would that I were dead!'

Her tears fell with the dews at even;
    Her tears fell ere the dews were dried;
She could not look on the sweet heaven,
    Either at morn or eventide.
After the flitting of the bats,
    When thickest dark did trance the sky,
    She drew her casement-curtain by,
And glanced athwart the glooming flats.
        She only said, 'The night is dreary,
            He cometh not,' she said;
        She said, 'I am aweary, aweary,
            I would that I were dead!'

Upon the middle of the night,
    Waking she heard the night-fowl crow:
The cock sung out an hour ere light:
    From the dark fen the oxen's low

Came to her: without hope of change,
   In sleep she seem'd to walk forlorn,
   Till cold winds woke the gray-eyed morn
About the lonely moated grange.
      She only said, 'The day is dreary,
        He cometh not,' she said;
      She said, 'I am aweary, aweary,
        I would that I were dead!'

About a stone-cast from the wall
   A sluice with blacken'd waters slept,
And o'er it many, round and small,
   The cluster'd marish-mosses crept.
Hard by a poplar shook alway,
   All silver-green with gnarlèd bark:
   For leagues no other tree did mark
The level waste, the rounding gray.
      She only said, 'My life is dreary,
        He cometh not,' she said;
      She said, 'I am aweary, aweary,
        I would that I were dead!'

And ever when the moon was low,
   And the shrill winds were up and away,
In the white curtain, to and fro,
   She saw the gusty shadow sway.
But when the moon was very low,
   And wild winds bound within their cell,
   The shadow of the poplar fell
Upon her bed, across her brow.
      She only said, 'The night is dreary,
        He cometh not,' she said;
      She said, 'I am aweary, aweary,
        I would that I were dead!'

All day within the dreamy house,
   The doors upon their hinges creak'd;
The blue fly sung in the pane; the mouse
   Behind the mouldering wainscot shriek'd,

Or from the crevice peer'd about.
　　Old faces glimmer'd thro' the doors,
　　Old footsteps trod the upper floors,
　　Old voices called her from without.
　　　She only said, 'My life is dreary,
　　　　He cometh not,' she said;
　　　She said, 'I am aweary, aweary,
　　　　I would that I were dead!'

The sparrow's chirrup on the roof,
　　The slow clock ticking, and the sound
Which to the wooing wind aloof
　　The poplar made, did all confound
Her sense; but most she loathed the hour
　　When the thick-moted sunbeam lay
　　Athwart the chambers, and the day
Was sloping toward his western bower.
　　　Then, said she, 'I am very dreary,
　　　　He will not come,' she said;
　　　She wept, 'I am aweary, aweary,
　　　　Oh God, that I were dead!'

CHRISTINA G. ROSSETTI

Twilight Night, II

Where my heart is (wherever that may be)
  Might I but follow!
If you fly thither over heath and lea,
O honey-seeking bee,
  O careless swallow,
Bid some for whom I watch keep watch for me.

Alas! that we must dwell, my heart and I,
  So far asunder.
Hours wax to days, and days and days creep by;
I watch with wistful eye,
  I wait and wonder:
When will that day draw nigh – that hour draw nigh?

Not yesterday, and not I think today;
  Perhaps tomorrow.
Day after day 'tomorrow' thus I say:
I watched so yesterday
  In hope and sorrow,
Again today I watch the accustomed way.

ANNE MICHAELS

Three Weeks

Three weeks longing, water burning
stone. Three weeks leopard blood
pacing under the loud insomnia of stars.
Three weeks voltaic. Weeks of winter
afternoons, darkness half descended.
Howling at distance, ocean
pulling between us, bending time.
Three weeks finding you in me in new places,
luminescent as a tetra in depths,
its neon trail.
Three weeks shipwrecked on this mad island;
twisting aurora of perfumes. Every boundary of body
electrified, every thought hunted down
by memory of touch. Three weeks of open eyes
when you call, your first question,
Did I wake you . . .

ROBERT BROWNING

In Three Days

So, I shall see her in three days
And just one night, but nights are short,
Then two long hours, and that is morn.
See how I come, unchanged, unworn!
Feel, where my life broke off from thine,
How fresh the splinters keep and fine, –
Only a touch and we combine!

Too long, this time of year, the days!
But nights, at least the nights are short.
As night shows where her one moon is,
A hand's-breadth of pure light and bliss,
So life's night gives my lady birth
And my eyes hold her! What is worth
The rest of heaven, the rest of earth?

O loaded curls, release your store
Of warmth and scent, as once before
The tingling hair did, lights and darks
Outbreaking into fairy sparks,
When under curl and curl I pried
After the warmth and scent inside,
Through lights and darks how manifold –
The dark inspired, the light controlled!
As early Art embrowns the gold.

What great fear, should one say, 'Three days
That change the world might change as well
Your fortune; and if joy delays,
Be happy that no worse befell!'
What small fear, if another says,
'Three days and one short night beside
May throw no shadow on your ways;

But years must teem with change untried,
With chance not easily defied,
With an end somewhere undescried.'
No fear! – or if a fear be born
This minute, it dies out in scorn.
Fear? I shall see her in three days
And one night, now the nights are short,
Then just two hours, and that is morn.

ROBERT GRAVES

Not to Sleep

Not to sleep all the night long, for pure joy,
Counting no sheep and careless of chimes,
Welcoming the dawn confabulation
Of birds, her children, who discuss idly
Fanciful details of the promised coming –
Will she be wearing red, or russet, or blue,
Or pure white? – whatever she wears, glorious:
Not to sleep all the night long, for pure joy,
This is given to few but at last to me,
So that when I laugh and stretch and leap from bed
I shall glide downstairs, my feet brushing the carpet
In courtesy to civilized progression,
Though, did I wish, I could soar through the open window
And perch on a branch above, acceptable ally
Of the birds still alert, grumbling gently together.

ELIZABETH BISHOP

Invitation to Miss Marianne Moore

From Brooklyn, over the Brooklyn Bridge, on this fine
        morning,
    please come flying.
In a cloud of fiery pale chemicals,
    please come flying,
to the rapid rolling of thousands of small blue drums
descending out of the mackerel sky
over the glittering grandstand of harbor-water,
    please come flying.

Whistles, pennants and smoke are blowing. The ships
are signaling cordially with multitudes of flags
rising and falling like birds all over the harbor.
Enter: two rivers, gracefully bearing
countless little pellucid jellies
in cut-glass epergnes dragging with silver chains.
The flight is safe; the weather is all arranged.
The waves are running in verses this fine morning.
    Please come flying.

Come with the pointed toe of each black shoe
trailing a sapphire highlight,
with a black capeful of butterfly wings and bon-mots,
with heaven knows how many angels all riding
on the broad black brim of your hat,
    please come flying.

Bearing a musical inaudible abacus,
a slight censorious frown, and blue ribbons,
    please come flying.
Facts and skyscrapers glint in the tide; Manhattan
is all awash with morals this fine morning,
    so please come flying.

Mounting the sky with natural heroism,
above the accidents, above the malignant movies,
the taxicabs and injustices at large,
while horns are resounding in your beautiful ears
that simultaneously listen to
a soft uninvented music, fit for the musk deer,
      please come flying.

For whom the grim museums will behave
like courteous male bower-birds,
for whom the agreeable lions lie in wait
on the steps of the Public Library,
eager to rise and follow through the doors
up into the reading rooms,
      please come flying.
We can sit down and weep; we can go shopping,
or play at a game of constantly being wrong
with a priceless set of vocabularies,
or we can bravely deplore, but please
      please come flying.

With dynasties of negative constructions
darkening and dying around you,
with grammar that suddenly turns and shines
like flocks of sandpipers flying,
      please come flying.

Come like a light in the white mackerel sky,
come like a daytime comet
with a long unnebulous train of words,
from Brooklyn, over the Brooklyn Bridge, on this fine
      morning,
      please come flying.

MONIZA ALVI

A Bowl of Warm Air

Someone is falling towards you
as an apple falls from a branch,
moving slowly, imperceptibly as if
into a new political epoch,
or excitedly like a dog towards a bone.
He is holding in both hands
everything he knows he has –
a bowl of warm air.

He has sighted you from afar
as if you were a dramatic crooked tree
on the horizon and he has seen you close up
like the underside of a mushroom.
But he cannot open you like a newspaper
or put you down like a newspaper.

And you are satisfied that he is veering towards you
and that he is adjusting his speed
and that the sun and the wind and rain are in front of him
and the sun and the wind and rain are behind him.

JOHN MONTAGUE

All Legendary Obstacles

All legendary obstacles lay between
Us, the long imaginary plain,
The monstrous ruck of mountains
And, swinging across the night,
Flooding the Sacramento, San Joaquin,
The hissing drift of winter rain.

All day I waited, shifting
Nervously from station to bar
As I saw another train sail
By, the San Francisco Chief or
Golden Gate, water dripping
From great flanged wheels.

At midnight you came, pale
Above the negro porter's lamp.
I was too blind with rain
And doubt to speak, but
Reached from the platform
Until our chilled hands met.

You had been travelling for days
With an old lady, who marked
A neat circle on the glass
With her glove, to watch us
Move into the wet darkness
Kissing, still unable to speak.

Superlatively

WILLIAM SHAKESPEARE

Sonnet 130

My mistress' eyes are nothing like the sun;
Coral is far more red than her lips' red;
If snow be white, why then her breasts are dun;
If hairs be wires, black wires grow on her head.
I have seen roses damasked, red and white,
But no such roses see I in her cheeks,
And in some perfumes is there more delight
Than in the breath that from my mistress reeks.
I love to hear her speak, yet well I know
That music hath a far more pleasing sound.
I grant I never saw a goddess go;
My mistress when she walks treads on the ground.
   And yet, by heaven, I think my love as rare
   As any she belied with false compare.

IAN DUHIG

From the Irish

According to Dineen, a Gael unsurpassed
in lexicographical enterprise, the Irish
for moon means 'the white circle in a slice
of half-boiled potato or turnip'. A star
is the mark on the forehead of a beast
and the sun is the bottom of a lake, or well.

Well, if I say to you your face
is like a slice of half-boiled turnip,
your hair is the colour of a lake's bottom
and at the centre of each of your eyes
is the mark of the beast, it is because
I want to love you properly, according to Dineen.

BEN JONSON

from *A Celebration of Charis,*
in Ten Lyric Pieces

Her Triumph

See the chariot at hand here of Love,
  Wherein my lady rideth!
Each that draws is a swan or a dove,
  And well the car Love guideth.
As she goes, all hearts do duty
    Unto her beauty;
And enamour'd, do wish, so they might
    But enjoy such a sight,
That they still were to run by her side,
Through swords, through seas, whither she would ride.

Do but look on her eyes, they do light
  All that Love's world compriseth!
Do but look on her hair, it is bright
  As Love's star when it riseth!
Do but mark, her forehead's smoother
    Than words that soothe her!
And from her arched brows, such a grace
    Sheds itself through the face
As alone there triumphs to the life
All the gain, all the good, of the elements' strife.

Have you seen but a bright lily grow,
  Before rude hands have touch'd it?
Have you mark'd but the fall of the snow
  Before the soil hath smutch'd it?
Have you felt the wool of the beaver?
    Or swan's down ever?

Or have smelt of the bud of the briar?
　　Or the nard in the fire?
Or have tasted the bag of the bee?
Oh so white! Oh so soft! Oh so sweet is she!

THE KING JAMES BIBLE

from *The Song of Solomon*

My beloved is white and ruddy,
the chiefest among ten thousand.
His head is as the most fine gold,
his locks are bushy, and black as a raven.
His eyes are as the eyes of doves by the rivers of water,
washed with milk, and fitly set.
His cheeks are as a bed of spices, as sweet flowers:
his lips like lilies, dropping sweet-smelling myrrh.
His hands are as gold rings set with the beryl:
his belly is as bright ivory overlaid with sapphires.
His legs are as pillars of marble, set upon sockets of fine
　　gold:
his countenance is as Lebanon, excellent as the cedars.
His mouth is most sweet, yea, he is altogether lovely.

GEORGE GORDON, LORD BYRON

She Walks in Beauty

She walks in beauty, like the night
   Of cloudless climes and starry skies;
And all that's best of dark and bright
   Meet in her aspect and her eyes:
Thus mellow'd to that tender light
   Which heaven to gaudy day denies.

One shade the more, one ray the less,
   Had half impair'd the nameless grace
Which waves in every raven tress,
   Or softly lightens o'er her face;
Where thoughts serenely sweet express
   How pure, how dear their dwelling place.

And on that cheek, and o'er that brow,
   So soft, so calm, yet eloquent,
The smiles that win, the tints that glow,
   But tell of days in goodness spent,
A mind at peace with all below,
   A heart whose love is innocent!

AUSTIN CLARKE

The Planter's Daughter

When night stirred at sea
And the fire brought a crowd in,
They say that her beauty
Was music in mouth
And few in the candlelight
Thought her too proud,
For the house of the planter
Is known by the trees.

Men that had seen her
Drank deep and were silent,
The women were speaking
Wherever she went –
As a bell that is rung
Or a wonder told shyly,
And O she was the Sunday
In every week.

somewhere i have never travelled,gladly beyond
any experience,your eyes have their silence:
in your most frail gesture are things which enclose me,
or which i cannot touch because they are too near

your slightest look easily will unclose me
though i have closed myself as fingers,
you open always petal by petal myself as Spring opens
(touching skilfully,mysteriously)her first rose

or if your wish be to close me,i and
my life will shut very beautifully,suddenly,
as when the heart of this flower imagines
the snow carefully everywhere descending;

nothing which we are to perceive in this world equals
the power of your intense fragility:whose texture
compels me with the colour of its countries,
rendering death and forever with each breathing

(i do not know what it is about you that closes
and opens;only something in me understands
the voice of your eyes is deeper than all roses)
nobody,not even the rain,has such small hands

WILLIAM SHAKESPEARE

from *The Merchant of Venice*, V, i

LORENZO:
    The moon shines bright. In such a night as this,
    When the sweet wind did gently kiss the trees
    And they did make no noise, in such a night
    Troilus methinks mounted the Troyan walls,
    And sighed his soul toward the Grecian tents
    Where Cressid lay that night.

JESSICA: In such a night
    Did Thisbe fearfully o'ertrip the dew,
    And saw the lion's shadow ere himself,
    And ran dismayed away.

LORENZO: In such a night
    Stood Dido with a willow in her hand
    Upon the wild sea banks, and waft her love
    To come again to Carthage.

JESSICA: In such a night
    Medea gathered the enchanted herbs
    That did renew old Aeson.

LORENZO: In such a night
    Did Jessica steal from the wealthy Jew,
    And with an unthrift love did run from Venice
    As far as Belmont.

JESSICA: In such a night
    Did young Lorenzo swear he loved her well,
    Stealing her soul with many vows of faith,
    And ne'er a true one.

LORENZO: In such a night
    Did pretty Jessica, like a little shrew,
    Slander her love, and he forgave it her.

JESSICA:
    I would out-night you, did nobody come;
    But hark, I hear the footing of a man.

OGDEN NASH

Reprise

Geniuses of countless nations
Have told their love for generations
Till all their memorable phrases
Are common as goldenrod or daisies.
Their girls have glimmered like the moon,
Or shimmered like a summer noon,
Stood like lily, fled like fawn,
Now the sunset, now the dawn,
Here the princess in the tower
There the sweet forbidden flower.
Darling, when I look at you
Every aged phrase is new,
And there are moments when it seems
I've married one of Shakespeare's dreams.

Persuasively

Come. And Be My Baby

The highway is full of big cars
going nowhere fast
And folks is smoking anything that'll burn
Some people wrap their lives around a cocktail glass
And you sit wondering
where you're going to turn.
I got it.
Come. And be my baby.

Some prophets say the world is gonna end
    tomorrow
But others say we've got a week or two
The paper is full of every kind of blooming horror
And you sit wondering
What you're gonna do.
I got it.
Come. And be my baby.

JOHN KEATS

To Fanny

I cry your mercy, pity, love – ay, love!
   Merciful love that tantalizes not,
One-thoughted, never-wandering, guileless love,
   Unmasked, and being seen – without a blot!
O! let me have thee whole, – all, all, be mine!
   That shape, that fairness, that sweet minor zest
Of love, your kiss – those hands, those eyes divine,
   That warm, white, lucent, million-pleasured breast –
Yourself – your soul – in pity give me all,
   Withhold no atom's atom or I die;
Or living on perhaps, your wretched thrall,
   Forget, in the mist of idle misery,
Life's purposes – the palate of my mind
Losing its gust, and my ambition blind!

Against Platonic Love

'Tis true, fair Celia, that by thee I live;
That every kiss, and every fond embrace
Forms a new soul within me, and doth give
A balsam to the wound made by thy face.
    Yet still methinks I miss
      That bliss
    Which lovers dare not name,
    And only then described is
    When flame doth meet with flame.

Those favours which do bless me every day
Are yet but empty and platonical.
Think not to please your servants with half pay.
Good gamesters never stick to throw at all.
    Who can endure to miss
      That bliss
    Which lovers dare not name,
    And only then described is
    When flame doth meet with flame?

If all those sweets within you must remain,
Unknown and ne'er enjoyed, like hidden treasure,
Nature, as well as I, will lose her name,
And you as well as I lose youthful pleasure.
    We wrong ourselves to miss
      That bliss
    Which lovers dare not name,
    And only then described is
    When flame doth meet with flame.

Our souls which long have peeped at one another
Out of the narrow casements of our eyes
Shall now by love conducted meet together
In secret caverns, where all pleasure lies.
   There, there we shall not miss
      That bliss
   Which lovers dare not name,
   And only then described is
   When flame doth meet with flame.

ROBIN ROBERTSON

Trysts

meet me
where the sun goes down
meet me
in the cave, under the battleground
meet me
on the broken branch
meet me
in the shade, below the avalanche
meet me
under the witch's spell
meet me
tonight, in the wishing well
meet me
on the famine lawn
meet me
in the eye of the firestorm
meet me
in your best shoes
and your favourite dress
meet me
on your own, in the wilderness
meet me
as my lover, as my only friend
meet me
on the river bed

THOMAS CAREW

from *A Rapture*

I will enjoy thee now, my Celia, come,
And fly with me to Love's Elysium.
The giant, Honour, that keeps cowards out,
Is but a masquer, and the servile rout
Of baser subjects only bend in vain
To the vast idol; whilst the nobler train
Of valiant lovers daily sail between
The huge Colossus' legs, and pass unseen
Unto the blissful shore. Be bold and wise,
And we shall enter: the grim Swiss denies
Only to tame fools a passage, that not know
He is but form and only frights in show
The duller eyes that look from far; draw near
And thou shalt scorn what we were wont to fear.
We shall see how the stalking pageant goes
With borrow'd legs, a heavy load to those
That made and bear him; not, as we once thought,
The seed of gods, but a weak model wrought
By greedy men, that seek to enclose the common,
And within private arms empale free woman.
  Come, then, and mounted on the wings of Love
We'll cut the flitting air and soar above
The monster's head, and in the noblest seats
Of those blest shades quench and renew our heats.
There shall the queens of love and innocence,
Beauty and Nature, banish all offence
From our close ivy-twines; there I'll behold
Thy bared snow and thy unbraided gold;
There my enfranchised hand on every side
Shall o'er thy naked polish'd ivory slide.
No curtain there, though of transparent lawn,
Shall be before thy virgin-treasure drawn;

But the rich mine, to the enquiring eye
Exposed, shall ready still for mintage lie,
And we will coin young Cupids. There a bed
Of roses and fresh myrtles shall be spread,
Under the cooler shade of cypress groves;
Our pillows of the down of Venus' doves,
Whereon our panting limbs we'll gently lay,
In the faint respites of our active play:
That so our slumbers may in dreams have leisure
To tell the nimble fancy our past pleasure,
And so our souls, that cannot be embraced,
Shall the embraces of our bodies taste.
Meanwhile the bubbling stream shall court the shore,
Th' enamour'd chirping wood-choir shall adore
In varied tunes the deity of love;
The gentle blasts of western winds shall move
The trembling leaves, and through their close boughs breathe
Still music, whilst we rest ourselves beneath
Their dancing shade; till a soft murmur, sent
From souls entranced in amorous languishment,
Rouse us, and shoot into our veins fresh fire,
Till we in their sweet ecstasy expire.
    Then, as the empty bee that lately bore
Into the common treasure all her store,
Flies 'bout the painted field with nimble wing,
Deflow'ring the fresh virgins of the spring,
So will I rifle all the sweets that dwell
In my delicious paradise, and swell
My bag with honey, drawn forth by the power
Of fervent kisses from each spicy flower.
I'll seize the rose-buds in their perfumed bed,
The violet knots, like curious mazes spread
O'er all the garden, taste the ripen'd cherry,
The warm firm apple, tipp'd with coral berry:
Then will I visit with a wand'ring kiss
The vale of lilies and the bower of bliss;
And where the beauteous region doth divide
Into two milky ways, my lips shall slide

Down those smooth alleys, wearing as they go
A tract for lovers on the printed snow;
Thence climbing o'er the swelling Apennine,
Retire into thy grove of eglantine,
Where I will all those ravish'd sweets distil
Through Love's alembic, and with chemic skill
From the mix'd mass one sovereign balm derive,
Then bring that great elixir to thy hive.
 Now in more subtle wreaths I will entwine
My sinewy thighs, my legs and arms with thine;
Thou like a sea of milk shalt lie display'd,
Whilst I the smooth calm ocean invade
With such a tempest, as when Jove of old
Fell down on Danaë in a storm of gold;
Yet my tall pine shall in the Cyprian strait
Ride safe at anchor and unlade her freight:
My rudder with thy bold hand, like a tried
And skilful pilot, thou shalt steer, and guide
My bark into love's channel, where it shall
Dance, as the bounding waves do rise or fall.
Then shall thy circling arms embrace and clip
My willing body, and thy balmy lip
Bathe me in juice of kisses, whose perfume
Like a religious incense shall consume,
And send up holy vapours to those powers
That bless our loves and crown our sportful hours,
That with such halcyon calmness fix our souls
In steadfast peace, as no affright controls.
There, no rude sounds shake us with sudden starts;
No jealous ears, when we unrip our hearts,
Suck our discourse in; no observing spies
This blush, that glance traduce; no envious eyes
Watch our close meetings; nor are we betray'd
To rivals by the bribed chambermaid.
No wedlock bonds unwreathe our twisted loves,
We seek no midnight arbour, no dark groves
To hide our kisses: there, the hated name
Of husband, wife, lust, modest, chaste or shame,

Are vain and empty words, whose very sound
Was never heard in the Elysian ground.
All things are lawful there, that may delight
Nature or unrestrained appetite;
Like and enjoy, to will and act is one:
We only sin when Love's rites are not done.

BARNABE BARNES

Would I Were Changed

Jove, for Europa's love, took shape of bull,
And, for Callisto, played Diana's part,
And, in a golden shower, he filled full
The lap of Danaë with celestial art.
Would I were changed but to my mistress' gloves,
That those white lovely fingers I might hide,
That I might kiss those hands, which mine heart loves,
Or else, that chain of pearl, her neck's vain pride,
Made proud with her neck's veins, that I might fold
About that lovely neck, and her paps tickle,
Or her to compass, like a belt of gold,
Or that sweet wine, which down her throat doth trickle,
To kiss her lips, and lie next to her heart,
Run through her veins, and pass by pleasure's part.

ROBERT HERRICK

Upon Julia's Clothes

When as in silks my *Julia* goes,
    Then, then (me thinks) how sweetly flows
That liquefaction of her clothes.

Next, when I cast mine eyes and see
That brave Vibration each way free;
O how that glittering taketh me!

ANNE STEVENSON

Sous-entendu

Don't think

    that I don't know
    that as you talk to me
    the hand of your mind
    is inconspicuously
    taking off my stocking,
    moving in resourceful blindness
    up along my thigh.

Don't think
    that I don't know
    that you know
    everything I say
    is a garment.

JOHN DONNE

Elegy: To His Mistress Going to Bed

Come, madam, come; all rest my powers defy;
Until I labour, I in labour lie.
The foe oft-times having the foe in sight
Is tired with standing, though they never fight.
Off with that girdle, like heaven's zone glistering,
But a far fairer world encompassing.
Unpin that spangled breast-plate, which you wear
That th' eyes of busy fools may be stopped there.
Unlace yourself: for that harmonious chime
Tells me from you that now 'tis your bed-time.
Off with that happy busk whom I envy
That still can be, and still can stand so nigh.
Your gown's going off such beauteous state reveals
As when from flow'ry meads th' hill's shadow steals.
Off with your wiry coronet, and show
The hairy diadem which on you doth grow.
Now off with those shoes, and then safely tread
In this love's hallowed temple, this soft bed.
In such white robes heaven's angels used to be
Received by men: thou, angel, bring'st with thee
A heaven like Mohammed's paradise; and though
Ill spirits walk in white, we easily know
By this these angels from an evil sprite:
They set our hairs, but these the flesh upright.
Licence my roving hands, and let them go
Behind, before, above, between, below.
Oh my America, my new-found land,
My kingdom, safeliest when with one man manned,
My mine of precious stones, my empery;
How blest am I in this discovering thee!
To enter in these bonds is to be free;
Then where my hand is set, my seal shall be,
Full nakedness, all joys are due to thee;

As souls unbodied, bodies unclothed must be,
To taste whole joys. Gems which you women use
Are as Atlanta's balls cast in men's views,
That when a fool's eye lighteth on a gem
His earthly soul may covet theirs, not them.
Like pictures, or like books' gay coverings, made
For laymen, are all women thus arrayed,
Themselves are mystic books, which only we
Whom their imputed grace will dignify
Must see revealed. Then since I may know,
As liberally as to a midwife show
Thyself. Cast all, yea, this white linen hence;
There is no penance, much less innocence.
To teach thee I am naked first: why then,
What needst thou have more covering than a man?

EDWARD THOMAS

Will you come?

Will you come?
Will you come?
Will you ride
So late
At my side?
O, will you come?

Will you come?
Will you come
If the night
Has a moon,
Full and bright?
O, will you come?

Would you come?
Would you come?
If the noon
Gave light,
Not the moon?
Beautiful, would you come?

Would you have come?
Would you have come
Without scorning,
Had it been
Still morning?
Beloved, would you have come?

If you come
Haste and come.
Owls have cried;
It grows dark
To ride.
Beloved, beautiful, come.

Passionately

And is it night? are they thine eyes that shine?
   Are we alone, and here? and here, alone?
May I come near, may I but touch thy shrine?
   Is jealousy asleep, and is he gone?
O Gods, no more! silence my lips with thine!
Lips, kisses, joys, hap, – blessings most divine!

Oh, come, my dear! our griefs are turned to night,
   And night to joys; night blinds pale envy's eyes;
Silence and sleep prepare us our delight;
   Oh, cease we then our woes, our griefs, our cries:
Oh, vanish words! words do but passions move;
O dearest life! joy's sweet! O sweetest love!

ROBERT BROWNING

Now

Out of your whole life give but a moment!
All of your life that has gone before,
All to come after it, – so you ignore,
So you make perfect the present, – condense,
In a rapture of rage, for perfection's endowment,
Thought and feeling and soul and sense –
Merged in a moment which gives me at last
You around me for once, you beneath me, above me –
Me – sure that despite of time future, time past, –
This tick of our life-time's one moment you love me!
How long such suspension may linger? Ah, Sweet –
The moment eternal – just that and no more –
When ecstasy's utmost we clutch at the core
While cheeks burn, arms open, eyes shut and lips meet!

JACKIE KAY

High Land

I don't remember who kissed who first,
who touched who first, who anything to whom.
All I remember in the highland night –
the sheep loose outside,
the full moon smoking in the sky –
was that you led me and I led you.
And all of a sudden we were in a small room
in a big house with the light coming in
and your legs open; mine too.
And it was this swirling, twirling thing.
It's hard to fasten it down;
it is hard to remember what was what –
who was who when the wind was coming in.

GEORGE GORDON, LORD BYRON

from *Don Juan*, Canto II

CLXXXVI

A long, long kiss, a kiss of youth, and love,
    And beauty, all concentrating like rays
Into one focus, kindled from above;
    Such kisses as belong to early days,
Where heart, and soul, and sense, in concert move,
    And the blood's lava, and the pulse a blaze,
Each kiss a heart-quake, – for a kiss's strength,
I think, it must be reckon'd by its length.

CLXXXVII

By length I mean duration; theirs endured
    Heaven knows how long – no doubt they never
        reckon'd;
And if they had, they could not have secured
    The sum of their sensations to a second:
They had not spoken; but they felt allured,
    As if their souls and lips each other beckon'd,
Which, being join'd, like swarming bees they clung –
Their hearts the flowers from whence the honey sprung.

CLXXXVIII

They were alone, but not alone as they
    Who shut in chambers think it loneliness;
The silent ocean, and the starlight bay,
    The twilight glow, which momently grew less,
The voiceless sands, and dropping caves, that lay
    Around them, made them to each other press,
As if there were no life beneath the sky
Save theirs, and that their life could never die.

They fear'd no eyes nor ears on that lone beach,
 They felt no terrors from the night, they were
All in all to each other: though their speech
 Was broken words, they *thought* a language there, –
And all the burning tongues the passions teach
 Found in one sigh the best interpreter
Of nature's oracle – first love, – that all
Which Eve has left her daughters since her fall.

EMILY DICKINSON

Come slowly – Eden!
Lips unused to Thee –
Bashful – sip thy Jessamines –
As the fainting Bee –

Reaching late his flower,
Round her chamber hums –
Counts his nectars –
Enters – and is lost in Balms.

HUGO WILLIAMS

Rhetorical Questions

How do you think I feel
when you make me talk to you
and won't let me stop
till the words turn into a moan?
Do you think I mind
when you put your hand over my mouth
and tell me not to move
so you can 'hear' it happening?

And how do you think I like it
when you tell me what to do
and your mouth opens
and you look straight through me?
Do you think I mind
when the blank expression comes
and you set off alone
down the hall of collapsing columns?

JO SHAPCOTT

Muse

When I kiss you in all the folding places
of your body, you make that noise like a dog
dreaming, dreaming of the long run he makes
in answer to some jolt to his hormones,
running across landfills, running, running
by tips and shorelines from the scent of too much,
but still going with head up and snout
in the air because he loves it all
and has to get away. I have to kiss deeper
and more slowly – your neck, your inner arm,
the neat creases under your toes, the shadow
behind your knee, the white angles of your groin –
until you fall quiet because only then
can I get the damned words to come into my mouth.

from *Epipsychidion*

Our breath shall intermix, our bosoms bound,
And our veins beat together; and our lips
With other eloquence than words, eclipse
The soul that burns between them and the wells
Which boil under our being's inmost cells,
The fountains of our deepest life, shall be
Confused in passion's golden purity,
As mountain-springs under the morning Sun.
We shall become the same, we shall be one
Spirit within two frames, oh! wherefore two?
One passion in twin-hearts, which grows and grew,
Till, like two meteors of expanding flame,
Those spheres instinct with it become the same,
Touch, mingle, are transfigured; ever still
Burning, yet ever inconsumable:
In one another's substance finding food,
Like flames too pure and light and unimbued
To nourish their bright lives with baser prey,
Which point to Heaven and cannot pass away:
One hope within two wills, one will beneath
Two overshadowing minds, one life, one death,
One Heaven, one Hell, one immortality,
And one annihilation!

THOM GUNN

The Bed

The pulsing stops where time has been,
  The garden is snow-bound,
The branches weighed down and the paths filled in,
  Drifts quilt the ground.

We lie soft-caught, still now it's done,
  Loose-twined across the bed
Like wrestling statues; but it still goes on
  Inside my head.

ELIZABETH JENNINGS

Passion

The violence is over. They lie apart,
They are shapes belonging to no-one or could be
Part of an abstract painting or figure sliding
Upon a Dali sea.
But they are breathing fast still as if they'd been running,
Man and woman, carried by a wind blowing
Out of an open window. Here is passion
Appeased, here is pleasure
Exulted in. And here
Is possible creation. Here could be
Adam and Eve, turning away ashamed.
Here is loss waiting to be redeemed.

MICHAEL DONAGHY

Pentecost

The neighbours hammered on the walls all night,
Outraged by the noise we made in bed.
Still we kept it up until by first light
We'd said everything that could be said.

Undaunted, we began to mewl and roar
As if desire had stripped itself of words.
Remember when we made those sounds before?
When we built a tower heavenwards
They were our reward for blasphemy.
And then again, two thousand years ago,
We huddled in a room in Galilee
Speaking languages we didn't know,
While amethyst uraeuses of flame
Hissed above us. We recalled the tower
And the tongues. We knew this was the same,
But love had turned the curse into a power.

See? It's something that we've always known:
Though we command the language of desire,
The voice of ecstasy is not our own.
We long to lose ourselves amid the choir
Of the salmon twilight and the mackerel sky,
The very air we take into our lungs,
And the rhododendron's cry.

And when you lick the sweat along my thigh,
Dearest, we renew the gift of tongues.

W. H. AUDEN

Lullaby

Lay your sleeping head, my love,
Human on my faithless arm;
Time and fevers burn away
Individual beauty from
Thoughtful children, and the grave
Proves the child ephemeral:
But in my arms till break of day
Let the living creature lie,
Mortal, guilty, but to me
The entirely beautiful.

Soul and body have no bounds:
To lovers as they lie upon
Her tolerant enchanted slope
In their ordinary swoon,
Grave the vision Venus sends
Of supernatural sympathy,
Universal love and hope;
While an abstract insight wakes
Among the glaciers and the rocks
The hermit's carnal ecstasy.

Certainty, fidelity
On the stroke of midnight pass
Like vibrations of a bell
And fashionable madmen raise
Their pedantic boring cry:
Every farthing of the cost,
All the dreaded cards foretell,
Shall be paid, but from this night
Not a whisper, not a thought,
Not a kiss nor look be lost.

Beauty, midnight, vision dies:
Let the winds of dawn that blow
Softly round your dreaming head
Such a day of welcome show
Eye and knocking heart may bless,
Find our mortal world enough;
Noons of dryness find you fed
By the involuntary powers,
Nights of insult let you pass
Watched by every human love.

SIMON ARMITAGE

Let me put it this way:
if you came to lay

your sleeping head
against my arm or sleeve,

and if my arm went dead,
or if I had to take my leave

at midnight, I should rather
cleave it from the joint or seam

than make a scene
or bring you round.

There,
how does that sound?

GAVIN EWART

Creation Myth Haiku

After the First Night
the Sun kissed the Moon: 'Darling,
you were wonderful!'

The morning after

LESLÉA NEWMAN

Possibly

to wake and find you sitting up in bed
with your black hair and gold skin
leaning against the white wall
a perfect slant of sunlight slashed
across your chest as if God
were Rembrandt or maybe Ingmar Bergman
but luckily it's too early to go to the movies
and all the museums are closed on Tuesday
anyway I'd rather be here with you
than in New York or possibly Amsterdam
with our eyes and lips and legs and bellies
and the sun as big as a house in the sky
and five minutes left before the world begins

JOHN DONNE

The Sun Rising

Busy old fool, unruly sun,
        Why dost thou thus,
Through windows, and through curtains call on us?
Must to thy motions lovers' seasons run?
        Saucy pedantic wretch, go chide
        Late schoolboys, and sour prentices,
    Go tell court-huntsmen, that the King will ride,
    Call country ants to harvest offices;
Love, all alike, no season knows, nor clime,
Nor hours, days, months, which are the rags of time.

        Thy beams, so reverend, and strong
        Why shouldst thou think?
I could eclipse and cloud them with a wink,
But that I would not lose her sight so long:
        If her eyes have not blinded thine,
        Look, and tomorrow late, tell me,
    Whether both th'Indias of spice and mine
    Be where thou left'st them, or lie here with me.
Ask for those kings whom thou saw'st yesterday,
And thou shalt hear, All here in one bed lay.

        She is all states, and all princes, I,
        Nothing else is.
Princes do but play us; compared to this,
All honour's mimic; all wealth alchemy.
        Thou sun art half as happy as we,
        In that the world's contracted thus;
    Thine age asks ease, and since thy duties be
    To warm the world, that's done in warming us.
Shine here to us, and thou art everywhere;
This bed thy centre is, these walls, thy sphere.

LOUIS MACNEICE

from *Trilogy for X*

II

And love hung still as crystal over the bed
    And filled the corners of the enormous room;
The boom of dawn that left her sleeping, showing
    The flowers mirrored in the mahogany table.

O my love, if only I were able
    To protract this hour of quiet after passion,
Not ration happiness but keep this door for ever
    Closed on the world, its own world closed within it.

But dawn's waves trouble with the bubbling minute,
    The names of books come clear upon their shelves,
The reason delves for duty and you will wake
    With a start and go on living on your own.

The first train passes and the windows groan,
    Voices will hector and your voice become
A drum in tune with theirs, which all last night
    Like sap that fingered through a hungry tree
Asserted our one night's identity.

WILLIAM SHAKESPEARE

from *Romeo and Juliet*, III, v

JULIET:
Wilt thou be gone? It is not yet near day.
It was the nightingale, and not the lark,
That pierced the fearful hollow of thine ear.
Nightly she sings on yond pomegranate tree.
Believe me, love, it was the nightingale.

ROMEO:
It was the lark, the herald of the morn;
No nightingale. Look, love, what envious streaks
Do lace the severing clouds in yonder East.
Night's candles are burnt out, and jocund day
Stands tiptoe on the misty mountain tops.
I must be gone and live, or stay and die.

JULIET:
Yond light is not daylight; I know it, I.
It is some meteor that the sun exhales
To be to thee this night a torchbearer
And light thee on thy way to Mantua.
Therefore stay yet. Thou needest not to be gone.

ROMEO:
Let me be ta'en, let me be put to death.
I am content, so thou wilt have it so.
I'll say yon grey is not the morning's eye;
'Tis but the pale reflex of Cynthia's brow.
Nor that is not the lark whose notes do beat
The vaulty heaven so high above our heads.
I have more care to stay than will to go.
Come, death, and welcome! Juliet wills it so.
How is't, my soul? Let's talk. It is not day.

JULIET:
It is, it is! Hie hence, be gone, away!
It is the lark that sings so out of tune,
Straining harsh discords and unpleasing sharps.

Some say the lark makes sweet division.
This doth not so, for she divideth us.
Some say the lark and loathèd toad change eyes.
O, now I would they had changed voices too,
Since arm from arm that voice doth us affray,
Hunting thee hence with hunt's-up to the day.
O, now be gone! More light and light it grows.

ROMEO:
More light and light: more dark and dark our woes.

PHILIP LARKIN

Talking in Bed

Talking in bed ought to be easiest,
Lying together there goes back so far,
An emblem of two people being honest.

Yet more and more time passes silently.
Outside, the wind's incomplete unrest
Builds and disperses clouds about the sky,

And dark towns heap up on the horizon.
None of this cares for us. Nothing shows why
At this unique distance from isolation

It becomes still more difficult to find
Words at once true and kind,
Or not untrue and not unkind.

Morning After

Sad how
Sunday morning finds us
separate after All,
side by side with nothing between us
but the Sunday papers.
Held like screens before us.
  Me, the Mirror
reflecting only on your closed profile.
  You, the Observer
encompassing larger, Other issues.
Without looking up
you ask me please to pass the colour section.
I shiver
while you flick too quickly
          too casually through the pages, with
          too passing
          an interest.

TENNESSEE WILLIAMS

Life Story

After you've been to bed together for the first time,
without the advantage or disadvantage of any prior
      acquaintance,
the other party very often says to you,
Tell me about yourself, I want to know all about you,
what's your story? And you think maybe they really and truly do

sincerely want to know your life story, and so you light up
a cigarette and begin to tell it to them, the two of you
lying together in completely relaxed positions
like a pair of rag dolls a bored child dropped on a bed.

You tell them your story, or as much of your story
as time or a fair degree of prudence allows, and they say,
    Oh, oh, oh, oh, oh,
each time a little more faintly, until the oh
is just an audible breath, and then of course

there's some interruption. Slow room service comes up
with a bowl of melting ice cubes, or one of you rises to pee
and gaze at himself with mild astonishment in the bathroom
      mirror.
And then, the first thing you know, before you've had time
to pick up where you left off with your enthralling life story,
they're telling you *their* life story, exactly as they'd intended to
      all along,

and you're saying, Oh, oh, oh, oh, oh,
each time a little more faintly, the vowel at last becoming
no more than an audible sigh,
as the elevator, halfway down the corridor and a turn to the
       left,
draws one last, long, deep breath of exhaustion
and stops breathing forever. Then?

Well, one of you falls asleep
and the other one does likewise with a lighted cigarette in his
       mouth,
and that's how people burn to death in hotel rooms.

WILLIAM SHAKESPEARE

Sonnet 129

The expense of spirit in a waste of shame
Is lust in action, and, till action, lust
Is perjured, murd'rous, bloody, full of blame,
Savage, extreme, rude, cruel, not to trust,
Enjoyed no sooner but despisèd straight,
Past reason hunted, and no sooner had,
Past reason hated as a swallowed bait
On purpose laid to make the taker mad;
Mad in pursuit, and in possession so,
Had, having, and in quest to have, extreme,
A bliss in proof, and proved, a very woe,
Before, a joy proposed, behind, a dream.
    All this the world well knows, yet none knows well
    To shun the heaven that leads men to this hell.

ELIZABETH BISHOP

Breakfast Song

My love, my saving grace,
your eyes are awfully blue.
I kiss your funny face,
your coffee-flavored mouth.
Last night I slept with you.
Today I love you so
how can I bear to go
(as soon I must, I know)
to bed with ugly death
in that cold, filthy place,
to sleep there without you,
without the easy breath
and nightlong, limblong warmth
I've grown accustomed to?
– Nobody wants to die;
tell me it is a lie!
But no, I know it's true.
It's just the common case;
there's nothing one can do.
My love, my saving grace,
your eyes are awfully blue
early and instant blue.

D. H. LAWRENCE

Gloire de Dijon

When she rises in the morning
I linger to watch her;
She spreads the bath-cloth underneath the window
And the sunbeams catch her
Glistening white on the shoulders,
While down her sides the mellow
Golden shadow glows as
She stoops to the sponge, and her swung breasts
Sway like full-blown yellow
Gloire de Dijon roses.

She drips herself with water, and her shoulders
Glisten as silver, they crumple up
Like wet and falling roses, and I listen
For the sluicing of their rain-dishevelled petals.
In the window full of sunlight
Concentrates her golden shadow
Fold on fold, until it glows as
Mellow as the glory roses.

OLIVIA MCCANNON

Ironing

You've just shaved and you smell of cream
I'm watching you press the metal point
Between buttons, over a collar, into a seam.

When you've left, I open the wardrobe quietly
I want to climb in and hang there with your shirts
With my creases, waiting for you to iron them out.

JOHN HEATH-STUBBS

The Unpredicted

The goddess Fortune be praised (on her toothed wheel
I have been mincemeat these several years)
Last night, for a whole night, the unpredictable
Lay in my arms, in a tender and unquiet rest –
(I perceived the irrelevance of my former tears) –
Lay, and at dawn departed. I rose and walked the streets,
Where a whitsuntide wind blew fresh, and blackbirds
Incontestably sang, and the people were beautiful.

Greedily

WILLIAM SHAKESPEARE

Sonnet 75

So are you to my thoughts as food to life,
Or as sweet seasoned showers are to the ground;
And for the peace of you I hold such strife
As 'twixt a miser and his wealth is found;
Now proud as an enjoyer, and anon
Doubting the filching age will steal his treasure;
Now counting best to be with you alone,
Then bettered that the world may see my pleasure;
Sometime all full with feasting on your sight,
And by and by clean starvèd for a look;
Possessing or pursuing no delight
Save what is had or must from you be took.
    Thus do I pine and surfeit day by day,
    Or gluttoning on all, or all away.

EDMUND SPENSER

from *Amoretti*

LXXVII

Was it a dream, or did I see it plain,
    a goodly table of pure ivory:
    all spread with junkets, fit to entertain,
    the greatest Prince with pompous royalty.
'Mongst which there in a silver dish did lie,
    two golden apples of unvalued price:
    far passing those which Hercules came by,
    or those which Atalanta did entice.
Exceeding sweet, yet void of sinful vice,
    that many sought yet none could ever taste,
    sweet fruit of pleasure brought from paradise:
    By Love himself and in his garden placed.
Her breast that table was so richly spread,
    my thoughts the guests, which would thereon have fed.

ROBERT HERRICK

Fresh Cheese and Cream

Would ye have fresh Cheese and Cream?
Julia's Breast can give you them:
And if more; Each Nipple cries,
To your Cream, here's Strawberries.

EDWIN MORGAN

Strawberries

There were never strawberries
like the ones we had
that sultry afternoon
sitting on the step
of the open french window
facing each other
your knees held in mine
the blue plates in our laps
the strawberries glistening
in the hot sunlight
we dipped them in sugar
looking at each other
not hurrying the feast
for one to come
the empty plates
laid on the stone together
with the two forks crossed
and I bent towards you
sweet in that air
in my arms
abandoned like a child
from your eager mouth
the taste of strawberries
in my memory
lean back again
let me love you

let the sun beat
on our forgetfulness
one hour of all
the heat intense
and summer lightning
on the Kilpatrick hills

let the storm wash the plates

HELEN DUNMORE

Wild Strawberries

What I get I bring home to you:
a dark handful, sweet-edged,
dissolving in one mouthful.

I bother to bring them for you
though they're so quickly over,
pulpless, sliding to juice,

a grainy rub on the tongue
and the taste's gone. If you remember
we were in the woods at wild strawberry time

and I was making a basket of dockleaves
to hold what you'd picked,
but the cold leaves unplaited themselves

and slid apart, and again unplaited themselves
until I gave up and ate wild strawberries
out of your hands for sweetness.

I lipped at your palm –
the little salt edge there,
the tang of money you'd handled.

As we stayed in the wood, hidden,
we heard the sound system below us
calling the winners at Chepstow,
faint as the breeze turned.

The sun came out on us, the shade blotches
went hazel: we heard names
bubble like stock-doves over the woods

as jockeys in stained silks gentled
those sweat-dark, shuddering horses
down to the walk.

CHRISTINA G. ROSSETTI

from *Goblin Market*

Morning and evening
Maids heard the goblins cry:
'Come buy our orchard fruits,
Come buy, come buy:
Apples and quinces,
Lemons and oranges,
Plump unpecked cherries,
Melons and raspberries,
Bloom-down-cheeked peaches,
Swart-headed mulberries,
Wild free-born cranberries,
Crab-apples, dewberries,
Pine-apples, blackberries,
Apricots, strawberries; –
All ripe together
In summer weather, –
Morns that pass by,
Fair eves that fly;
Come buy, come buy:
Our grapes fresh from the vine,
Pomegranates full and fine,
Dates and sharp bullaces,
Rare pears and greengages,
Damsons and bilberries,
Taste them and try:
Currants and gooseberries,
Bright-fire-like barberries,
Figs to fill your mouth,
Citrons from the South,
Sweet to tongue and sound to eye;
Come buy, come buy.'

Evening by evening
Among the brookside rushes,
Laura bowed her head to hear,
Lizzie veiled her blushes:
Crouching close together
In the cooling weather,
With clasping arms and cautioning lips,
With tingling cheeks and finger tips.
'Lie close,' Laura said,
Pricking up her golden head:
'We must not look at goblin men,
We must not buy their fruits:
Who knows upon what soil they fed
Their hungry thirsty roots?'
'Come buy,' call the goblins
Hobbling down the glen.
'Oh,' cried Lizzie, 'Laura, Laura,
You should not peep at goblin men.'
Lizzie covered up her eyes,
Covered close lest they should look;
Laura reared her glossy head,
And whispered like the restless brook:
'Look, Lizzie, look, Lizzie,
Down the glen tramp little men.
One hauls a basket,
One bears a plate,
One lugs a golden dish
Of many pounds weight.
How fair the vine must grow
Whose grapes are so luscious;
How warm the wind must blow
Thro' those fruit bushes.'
'No,' said Lizzie: 'No, no, no;
Their offers should not charm us,
Their evil gifts would harm us.'
She thrust a dimpled finger
In each ear, shut eyes and ran:
Curious Laura chose to linger
Wondering at each merchant man.

One had a cat's face,
One whisked a tail,
One tramped at a rat's pace,
One crawled like a snail,
One like a wombat prowled obtuse and furry,
One like a ratel tumbled hurry skurry.
She heard a voice like voice of doves
Cooing all together:
They sounded kind and full of loves
In the pleasant weather.

Laura stretched her gleaming neck
Like a rush-imbedded swan,
Like a lily from the beck,
Like a moonlit poplar branch,
Like a vessel at the launch
When its last restraint is gone.

JOHN DAVIES OF HEREFORD

The Author loving these homely meats specially, viz.: Cream, Pancakes, Buttered Pippin-pies (laugh, good people) and Tobacco; writ to that worthy and virtuous gentlewoman, whom he calleth Mistress, as followeth

If there were, oh! an Hellespont of cream
Between us, milk-white mistress, I would swim
To you, to show to both my love's extreme,
Leander-like, – yea! dive from brim to brim.
But met I with a buttered pippin-pie
Floating upon 't, that would I make my boat
To waft me to you without jeopardy,
Though sea-sick I might be while it did float.
Yet if a storm should rise, by night or day,
Of sugar-snows and hail of caraways,
Then, if I found a pancake in my way,
It like a plank should bring me to your kays;
  Which having found, if they tobacco kept,
  The smoke should dry me well before I slept.

from *Lifting Belly* (II)

Kiss my lips. She did.
Kiss my lips again she did.
Kiss my lips over and over and over again she did.
I have feathers.
Gentle fishes.
Do you think about apricots. We find them very beautiful.
    It is not alone their color it is their seeds that charm us.
    We find it a change.
Lifting belly is so strange.
I came to speak about it.
Selected raisins well their grapes grapes are good.
Change your name.
Question and garden.
It's raining. Don't speak about it.
My baby is a dumpling. I want to tell her something.
Wax candles. We have bought a great many wax candles.
    Some are decorated. They have not been lighted.
I do not mention roses.
Exactly.
Actually.
Question and butter.
I find the butter very good.
Lifting belly is so kind.
Lifting belly fattily.
Doesn't that astonish you.
You did want me.
Say it again.
Strawberry.
Lifting beside belly.
Lifting kindly belly.
Sing to me I say.
Some are wives not heroes.
Lifting belly merely.
Sing to me I say.

JOHN BERRYMAN

from *Dream Songs*: 4

Filling her compact & delicious body
with chicken páprika, she glanced at me
twice.
Fainting with interest, I hungered back
and only the fact of her husband & four other people
kept me from springing on her

or falling at her little feet and crying
'You are the hottest one for years of night
Henry's dazed eyes
have enjoyed, Brilliance.' I advanced upon
(despairing) my spumoni. – Sir Bones: is stuffed,
de world, wif feeding girls.

– Black hair, complexion Latin, jewelled eyes
downcast . . . The slob beside her   feasts . . . What wonders is
she sitting on, over there?
The restaurant buzzes. She might as well be on Mars.
Where did it all go wrong? There ought to be a law against
   Henry.
– Mr Bones: there is.

PAUL DURCAN

My Belovèd Compares Herself to a Pint of Stout

When in the heat of the first night of summer
I observe with a whistle of envy
That Jackson has driven out the road for a pint of stout,
She puts her arm around my waist and scolds me:
Am I not your pint of stout? Drink me.
There is nothing except, of course, self-pity
To stop you also having your pint of stout.

Putting self-pity on a leash in the back of the car,
I drive out the road, do a U-turn,
Drive in the hall door, up the spiral staircase,
Into her bedroom. I park at the foot of her bed,
Nonchalantly step out leaving the car unlocked,
Stroll over to the chest of drawers, lean on it,
Circumspectly inspect the backs of my hands,
Modestly request from her a pint of stout.
She turns her back, undresses, pours herself into bed,
Adjusts the pillows, slaps her hand on the coverlet:
Here I am – at the very least
Look at my new cotton nightdress before you shred it
And do not complain that I have not got a head on me.

I look around to see her foaming out of the bedclothes
Not laughing but gazing at me out of four-leggèd eyes.
She says: Close your eyes, put your hands around me.
I am the blackest, coldest pint you will ever drink
So sip me slowly, let me linger on your lips,
Ooze through your teeth, dawdle down your throat,
Before swooping down into your guts.

While you drink me I will deposit my scum
On your rim and when you get to the bottom of me,
No matter how hard you try to drink my dregs –
And being a man, you will, no harm in that –
I will keep bubbling up back at you.
For there is no escaping my aftermath.
Tonight – being the first night of summer –
You may drink as many pints of me as you like.
There are barrels of me in the tap room.
In thin daylight at nightfall,
You will fall asleep drunk on love.
When you wake early in the early morning
You will have a hangover,
All chaste, astringent, aflame with affirmation,
Straining at the bit to get to first mass
And holy communion and work – the good life.

Truly, madly, deeply

APHRA BEHN

Song

O Love! that stronger art than wine,
Pleasing delusion, witchery divine,
Wont to be prized above all wealth,
Disease that has more joys than health;
Though we blaspheme thee in our pain,
And of thy tyranny complain,
We are all bettered by thy reign.

What reason never can bestow
We to this useful passion owe;
Love wakes the dull from sluggish ease,
And learns a clown the art to please,
Humbles the vain, kindles the cold,
Makes misers free, and cowards bold;
'Tis he reforms the sot from drink,
And teaches airy fops to think.

When full brute appetite is fed,
And choked the glutton lies and dead,
Thou new spirits dost dispense
And 'finest the gross delights of sense:
Virtue's unconquerable aid
That against Nature can persuade,
And makes a roving mind retire
Within the bounds of just desire;
Cheerer of age, youth's kind unrest,
And half the heaven of the blest!

JOHN SKELTON

from *The Tunnyng of Elynour Rummynge*

'Behold,' she sayd, 'and se
How bright I am of ble!
Ich am not cast away,
That can my husband say,
Whan we kys and play
In lust and in lykyng.
He calleth me his whytyng,
His mullyng and his mytyng,
His nobbes and his conny,
His swetyng and his honny,
With, 'Bas, my prety bonny,
Thou art worth good and monny.'
This make I my falyre fonny,
Tyll that he dreme and dronny;
For, after all our sport,
Than wyll he rout and snort;
Than swetely togither we ly,
As two pygges in a sty.'

HUGO WILLIAMS

Nothing On

Alone at last
and plastered from the mini-bar
we were looking around
for something to amuse us
in the hotel room
when you fell upon
the Gideon Bible
in the bedside table
and made me read to you
from the Book of Genesis.

If you carry on
dancing round the room like that
in your sun-tan swim-suit
twirling the hotel's
complimentary fruitbowl
it won't be long
till the page fills up
with four-letter words
and I lose my place
in the story of the Creation.

ELIZABETH BARRETT BROWNING

from *Sonnets from the Portuguese*

XXIX

I think of thee! – my thoughts do twine and bud
About thee, as wild vines, about a tree,
Put out broad leaves, and soon there's nought to see
Except the straggling green which hides the wood.
Yet, O my palm-tree, be it understood
I will not have my thoughts instead of thee
Who art dearer, better! Rather, instantly
Renew thy presence! As a strong tree should,
Rustle thy boughs and set thy trunk all bare,
And let these bands of greenery which insphere thee,
Drop heavily down, . . . burst, shattered, everywhere!
Because, in this deep joy to see and hear thee
And breathe within thy shadow a new air,
I do not think of thee – I am too near thee.

DANTE GABRIEL ROSSETTI

Silent Noon

Your hands lie open in the long fresh grass, –
   The finger-points look through like rosy blooms:
   Your eyes smile peace. The pasture gleams and glooms
'Neath billowing skies that scatter and amass.
All around our nest, far as the eye can pass,
   Are golden kingcup-fields with silver edge
   Where the cow-parsley skirts the hawthorn-hedge.
'Tis visible silence, still as the hour-glass.

Deep in the sun-searched growths the dragon-fly
Hangs like a blue thread loosened from the sky: –
   So this wing'd hour is dropt to us from above.
Oh! clasp we to our hearts, for deathless dower,
This close-companioned inarticulate hour
   When twofold silence was the song of love.

JOHN FULLER

Valentine

The things about you I appreciate
  May seem indelicate:
I'd like to find you in the shower
And chase the soap for half an hour.
I'd like to have you in my power
  And see your eyes dilate.
I'd like to have your back to scour
And other parts to lubricate.
Sometimes I feel it is my fate
To chase you screaming up a tower
  Or make you cower
By asking you to differentiate
  Nietzsche from Schopenhauer.
I'd like successfully to guess your weight
  And win you at a fête.
I'd like to offer you a flower.

I like the hair upon your shoulders,
Falling like water over boulders.
I like the shoulders, too: they are essential.
Your collar-bones have great potential
(I'd like all your particulars in folders
  Marked *Confidential*).

I like your cheeks, I like your nose,
I like the way your lips disclose
The neat arrangement of your teeth
(Half above and half beneath)
  In rows.

I like your eyes, I like their fringes.
The way they focus on me gives me twinges.
Your upper arms drive me berserk.
I like the way your elbows work,
  On hinges.

I like your wrists, I like your glands,
I like the fingers on your hands.
I'd like to teach them how to count,
And certain things we might exchange,
Something familiar for something strange.
I'd like to give you just the right amount
  And get some change.

I like it when you tilt your cheek up.
I like the way you nod and hold a teacup.
I like your legs when you unwind them.
Even in trousers I don't mind them.
I like each softly-moulded kneecap.
I like the little crease behind them.
I'd always know, without a recap,
  Where to find them.

I like the sculpture of your ears.
I like the way your profile disappears
Whenever you decide to turn and face me.
I'd like to cross two hemispheres
  And have you chase me.
I'd like to smuggle you across frontiers
Or sail with you at night into Tangiers.
  I'd like you to embrace me.

I'd like to see you ironing your skirt
  And cancelling other dates.
I'd like to button up your shirt.
I like the way your chest inflates.
I'd like to soothe you when you're hurt
Or frightened senseless by invert-
  ebrates.

I'd like you even if you were malign
And had a yen for sudden homicide.
I'd let you put insecticide
  Into my wine.
I'd even like you if you were the Bride
  Of Frankenstein
Or something ghoulish out of Mamoulian's
  Jekyll and Hyde.
I'd even like you as my Julian
Of Norwich or Cathleen ni Houlihan.
  How melodramatic
If you were something muttering in attics
Like Mrs Rochester or a student of Boolean
Mathematics.

You are the end of self-abuse.
You are the eternal feminine.
I'd like to find a good excuse
To call on you and find you in.
I'd like to put my hand beneath your chin,
  And see you grin.
I'd like to taste your Charlotte Russe,
I'd like to feel my lips upon your skin,
I'd like to make you reproduce.

I'd like you in my confidence.
I'd like to be your second look.
I'd like to let you try the French Defence
  And mate you with my rook.
I'd like to be your preference
  And hence
I'd like to be around when you unhook.
I'd like to be your only audience,
The final name in your appointment book,
  Your future tense.

FRANK O'HARA

Having a Coke with You

is even more fun than going to San Sebastian, Irún, Hendaye, Biarritz,
    Bayonne
or being sick to my stomach on the Travesera de Gracia in Barcelona
partly because in your orange shirt you look like a better happier
    St Sebastian
partly because of my love for you, partly because of your love for
    yoghurt
partly because of the fluorescent orange tulips around the birches
partly because of the secrecy our smiles take on before people and
    statuary
it is hard to believe when I'm with you that there can be anything as
    still
as solemn as unpleasantly definitive as statuary when right in front of
    it
in the warm New York 4 o'clock light we are drifting back and forth
between each other like a tree breathing through its spectacles

and the portrait show seems to have no faces in it at all, just paint
you suddenly wonder why in the world anyone ever did them
                                                                    I look
at you and I would rather look at you than all the portraits in the
    world
except possibly for the *Polish Rider* occasionally and anyway it's in
    the Frick
which thank heavens you haven't gone to yet so we can go together
    the first time
and the fact that you move so beautifully more or less takes care of
    Futurism
just as at home I never think of the *Nude Descending a Staircase* or
at a rehearsal a single drawing of Leonardo or Michelangelo that used
    to wow me
and what good does all the research of the Impressionists do them

when they never got the right person to stand near the tree when the
    sun sank
or for that matter Marino Marini when he didn't pick the rider as
    carefully
as the horse
        it seems they were all cheated of some marvellous experience
which is not going to go wasted on me which is why I'm telling you
    about it

JOHN MILTON

from *Paradise Lost*, Book IV

With thee conversing I forget all time,
All seasons and their change, all please alike.
Sweet is the breath of morn, her rising sweet,
With charm of earliest birds; pleasant the sun
When first on this delightful land he spreads
His orient beams, on herb, tree, fruit, and flow'r,
Glist'ring with dew; fragrant the fertile earth
After soft showers; and sweet the coming on
Of grateful ev'ning mild, then silent night
With this her solemn bird and this fair moon,
And these the gems of heav'n, her starry train:
But neither breath of morn when she ascends
With charm of earliest birds, nor rising sun
On this delightful land, nor herb, fruit, flow'r,
Glist'ring with dew, nor fragrance after showers,
Nor grateful ev'ning mild, nor silent night
With this her solemn bird, nor walk by moon,
Or glittering starlight without thee is sweet.

THOMAS CAMPION

O sweet delight, O more than human bliss,
With her to live that ever loving is!
To hear her speak whose words so well are placed,
That she by them, as they in her, are graced;
Those looks to view that feast the viewer's eye,
How blest is he that may so live and die!

Such love as this the golden times did know,
When all did reap, yet none took care to sow.
Such love as this an endless summer makes,
And all distaste from frail affection takes.
So loved, so blest in my beloved am I,
Which till their eyes ache, let iron men envy.

ADRIAN MITCHELL

Celia Celia

When I am sad and weary
When I think all hope has gone
When I walk along High Holborn
I think of you with nothing on

WALT WHITMAN

When I Heard at the Close of the Day

When I heard at the close of the day how my name had been
    receiv'd with plaudits in the capitol, still it was not a happy
    night for me that follow'd,
And else when I carous'd, or when my plans were accomplish'd,
    still I was not happy,
But the day when I rose at dawn from the bed of perfect health,
    refresh'd, singing, inhaling the ripe breath of autumn,
When I saw the full moon in the west grow pale and disappear in
    the morning light,
When I wander'd alone over the beach, and undressing bathed,
    laughing with the cool waters, and saw the sun rise,
And when I thought how my dear friend my lover was on his
    way coming, O then I was happy,
O then each breath tasted sweeter, and all that day my food
    nourish'd me more, and the beautiful day pass'd well,
And the next came with equal joy, and with the next at evening
    came my friend,
And that night while all was still I heard the waters roll slowly
    continually up the shores,
I heard the hissing rustle of the liquid and sands as directed to me
    whispering to congratulate me,
For the one I love most lay sleeping by me under the same cover
    in the cool night,
In the stillness in the autumn moonbeams his face was inclined
    toward me,
And his arm lay lightly around my breast – and that night I was
    happy.

WILFRED OWEN

From My Diary, July 1914

Leaves
  Murmuring by myriads in the shimmering trees.
Lives
  Wakening with wonder in the Pyrenees.
Birds
  Cheerily chirping in the early day.
Bards
  Singing of summer, scything through the hay.
Bees
  Shaking the heavy dews from bloom and frond.
Boys
  Bursting the surface of the ebony pond.
Flashes
  Of swimmers carving through the sparkling cold.
Fleshes
  Gleaming with wetness to the morning gold.
A mead
  Bordered about with warbling waterbrooks.
A maid
  Laughing the love-laugh with me; proud of looks.
The heat
  Throbbing between the upland and the peak.
Her heart
  Quivering with passion to my pressèd cheek.
Braiding
  Of floating flames across the mountain brow.
Brooding
  Of stillness; and a sighing of the bough.
Stirs
  Of leaflets in the gloom; soft petal-showers;
Stars
  Expanding with the starr'd nocturnal flowers.

THOMAS HOOD

It was not in the winter
  Our loving lot was cast!
It was the time of roses,
  We plucked them as we passed!

That churlish season never frowned
  On early lovers yet! –
Oh no – the world was newly crowned
  With flowers, when first we met.

'Twas twilight, and I bade you go,
  But still you held me fast; –
It was the time of roses, –
  We plucked them as we passed!

What else could peer my glowing cheek
  That tears began to stud? –
And when I asked the like of Love
  You snatched a damask bud, –

And oped it to the dainty core
  Still glowing to the last: –
It was the time of roses,
  We plucked them as we passed!

ROGER MCGOUGH

from *Summer with Monika*

they say the sun shone now and again
but it was generally cloudy
with far too much rain

they say babies were born
married couples made love
(often with eachother)
and people died
(sometimes violently)

they say it was an average
                    ordinary
                    moderate
                    run of the mill
                    commonorgarden
                    summer
. . . but it wasn't

for i locked a yellowdoor
and i threw away the key
and i spent summer with monika
and monika spent summer with me

unlike everybody else
we made friends with the weather . . .
mostdays the sun called
                    and sprawled
allover the place

or the wind blew in
as breezily as ever
and ran its fingers through our hair
but usually
it was the moon that kept us company

somedays we thought about the seaside
and built sandcastles on the blankets
and paddled in the pillows
or swam in the sink
and played with the shoals of dishes

otherdays we went for long walks
around the table
and picnicked on the banks
of the settee
or just sunbathed lazily
in front of the fire
until the shilling set on the horizon

we danced a lot that summer . . .
bosanovaed by the bookcase
or maddisoned instead
hulligullied by the oven
or twisted round the bed

at first we kept birds
in a transistor box
to sing for us
but sadly they died
we being too embraced in eachother
to feed them

but it didn't really matter
because we made lovesongs with our bodies
i became the words
and she put me to music

they say it was just
                 like
                 anyother
                 summer
                 . . . but it wasn't
for we had love and eachother
and the moon for company
when i spent summer with monika
and
         monika
             spent summer
                 with me.

When to my deadly pleasure,
When to my lively torment,
Lady mine eyes remained,
Joined alas to your beams,

With violence of heav'nly
Beauty tied to virtue,
Reason abashed retired,
Gladly my senses yielded.

Gladly my senses yielding,
Thus to betray my heart's fort,
Left me devoid of all life;

They to the beamy Suns went,
Where by the death of all deaths,
Find to what harm they hastened,

Like to the silly *Sylvan*,
Burn'd by the light he best liked,
When with a fire he first met.

Yet, yet, a life to their death,
Lady you have reserved,
Lady the life of all love;

For though my sense be from me,
And I be dead who want sense,
Yet do we both live in you.

Turned anew by your means,
Unto the flower that ay turns,
As you, alas, my Sun bends;

Thus do I fall to rise thus,
Thus do I die to live thus,
Changed to a change, I change not.

Thus may I not be from you:
Thus be my senses on you:
Thus what I think is of you:
Thus what I seek is in you:
    All what I am, it is you!

A. D. HOPE

A Blason

My foundling, my fondling, my frolic first-footer,
My circler, my sidler, shy-sayer yes-and-no,
Live-levin, light-looker, darter and doubter,
Pause of perhaps in my turvey of touch-and-go;

My music, my mandrake, merrythought to my marrow-bone,
Tropic to my true-pole and ripe to my rich,
Wonderer, wanderer, walker-in-wood-alone,
Eye-asker, acher, angel-with-an-itch;

My tittup, my tansy, tease-tuft in tumble-toil,
My frisker, my fettler, trickster and trier,
Knick-knacker, knee-knocker, cleaver in kindle-coil,
My handler, my honeysuckler, phoenix-on-fire;

My cunny, my cracker-jack, my cantrip, my kissing-crust,
Rock-rump and wring-rib in wrestle of randy-bout,
Lithe-lier, limber-leg, column of counter-thrust,
My heave-horn, my hyphener, dew-dealer in-and-out;

My, ah, my rough-rider now; my, oh, my deep-driver,
Burly-bags, bramble-ball, brace-belly, bruise-bud,
Shuttle-cock, slow-shagger, sweet-slugger, swift-swiver,
My, YES now and yes NOW – rip, river and flood!

My breacher, my broacher, my burst-boy, my bubblyjock,
My soberer, slacken-soon, numb-nub and narrower,
My wrinkler, my rumplet, prim-purse of poppycock,
Slither-slot, shrivel-shaft, shrinker and sorrower;

My soft-sigher, snuggle-snake, sleeper and slaker,
My dandler, my deft-dear, dreamer of double-deal,
And, oh, my wry-writher, my worker and waker,
Stirrer and stander now, fledge to my feel;

My prodigy, prodigal, palindrome of pleasure,
Rise-ripe and rive-rose, rod of replevin,
Now furrow my fallow, now trench to my treasure,
Harvester, harbinger, harrow my heaven.

WILLIAM SHAKESPEARE

from *A Midsummer Night's Dream*, V, i

HIPPOLYTA:
   'Tis strange, my Theseus, that these lovers speak of.
THESEUS:
   More strange than true. I never may believe
   These antique fables, nor these fairy toys.
   Lovers and madmen have such seething brains,
   Such shaping fantasies, that apprehend
   More than cool reason ever comprehends.
   The lunatic, the lover, and the poet
   Are of imagination all compact:
   One sees more devils than vast hell can hold;
   That is the madman: the lover, all as frantic,
   Sees Helen's beauty in a brow of Egypt:
   The poet's eye, in a fine frenzy rolling,
   Doth glance from heaven to earth, from earth to heaven;
   And as imagination bodies forth
   The forms of things unknown, the poet's pen
   Turns them to shapes, and gives to airy nothing
   A local habitation and a name.
   Such tricks hath strong imagination,
   That if it would but apprehend some joy,
   It comprehends some bringer of that joy:
   Or, in the night, imagining some fear,
   How easy is a bush suppos'd a bear!

THOMAS MIDDLETON

Love is like a lamb, and love is like a lion;
Fly from love, he fights; fight, then does he fly on;
Love is all in fire, and yet is ever freezing;
Love is much in winning, yet is more in leezing;
Love is ever sick, and yet is never dying;
Love is ever true, and yet is ever lying;
Love does dote in liking, and is mad in loathing;
Love indeed is anything, yet indeed is nothing.

PIET HEIN

What Love Is Like

Love is like
a pineapple,
sweet and
undefinable.

From a distance

ROBERT BURNS

A Red, Red Rose

My luve is like a red, red rose,
    That's newly sprung in June:
My luve is like the melodie,
    That's sweetly play'd in tune.
As fair art thou, my bonie lass,
    So deep in luve am I,
And I will luve thee still, my dear,
    Till a' the seas gang dry.

Till a' the seas gang dry, my dear,
    And the rocks melt wi' the sun!
And I will luve thee still, my dear,
    While the sands o' life shall run.
And fare-thee-weel, my only luve,
    And fare-thee-weel a while!
And I will come again, my luve,
    Tho' it were ten-thousand mile.

E. B. WHITE

Natural History

(A Letter to Katharine, from the King Edward Hotel, Toronto)

The spider, dropping down from twig,
Unwinds a thread of her devising:
A thin, premeditated rig
To use in rising.

And all the journey down through space,
In cool descent, and loyal-hearted,
She builds a ladder to the place
From which she started.

Thus I, gone forth, as spiders do,
In spider's web a truth discerning,
Attach one silken strand to you
For my returning.

EDWIN MORGAN

One Cigarette

No smoke without you, my fire.
After you left,
your cigarette glowed on in my ashtray
and sent up a long thread of such quiet grey
I smiled to wonder who would believe its signal
of so much love. One cigarette
in the non-smoker's tray.
As the last spire
trembles up, a sudden draught
blows it winding into my face.
Is it smell, is it taste?
You are here again, and I am drunk on your tobacco lips.
Out with the light.
Let the smoke lie back in the dark.
Till I hear the very ash
sigh down among the flowers of brass
I'll breathe, and long past midnight, your last kiss.

JOHN CLARE

To Mary

I sleep with thee, and wake with thee,
And yet thou art not there;
I fill my arms with thoughts of thee,
And press the common air.
Thy eyes are gazing upon mine,
When thou art out of sight;
My lips are always touching thine,
At morning, noon, and night.

I think and speak of other things
To keep my mind at rest:
But still to thee my memory clings
Like love in woman's breast.
I hide it from the world's wide eye
And think and speak contrary;
But soft the wind comes from the sky,
And whispers tales of Mary.

The night wind whispers in my ear,
The moon shines in my face;
A burden still of chilling fear
I find in every place.
The breeze is whispering in the bush,
And the dews fall from the tree,
All, sighing on, and will not hush
Some pleasant tales of thee.

ANONYMOUS

My love is faren in a land;
Alas why is she so?
And I am so sore bound
I may not come her to.
She hath my heart in hold
Wherever she ride or go,
With true love a thousandfold.

ANONYMOUS

Westron wind, when will thou blow,
The small rain down can rain?
Christ if my love were in my arms,
And I in my bed again.

EDMUND SPENSER

from *Amoretti*

LXXVIII

Lacking my love I go from place to place,
    like a young fawn that late hath lost the hind;
    and seek each where, where last I saw her face,
    whose image yet I carry fresh in mind.
I seek the fields with her late footing signed,
    I seek her bower with her late presence decked.
    yet nor in field nor bower I her can find;
    yet field and bower are full of her aspect.
But when my eyes I thereunto direct,
    then idly back return to me again,
    and when I hope to see there true object,
    I find my self but fed with fancies vain.
Cease then, my eyes, to seek her self to see,
    and let my thoughts behold her self in me.

MATTHEW ARNOLD

To Marguerite – Continued

Yes! in the sea of life enisled,
With echoing straits between us thrown,
Dotting the shoreless watery wild,
We mortal millions live *alone*.
The islands feel the enclasping flow,
And then their endless bounds they know.

But when the moon their hollows lights,
And they are swept by balms of spring,
And in their glens, on starry nights,
The nightingales divinely sing;
And lovely notes, from shore to shore,
Across the sounds and channels pour –

Oh! then a longing like despair
Is to their farthest caverns sent;
For surely once, they feel, we were
Parts of a single continent!
Now round us spreads the watery plain –
Oh might our marges meet again!

Who order'd, that their longing's fire
Should be, as soon as kindled, cool'd?
Who renders vain their deep desire? –
A God, a God their severance ruled!
And bade betwixt their shores to be
The unplumb'd, salt, estranging sea.

ANDREW MARVELL

The Definition of Love

My love is of a birth as rare
As 'tis for object strange and high:
It was begotten by Despair
Upon Impossibility.

Magnanimous Despair alone
Could show me so divine a thing,
Where feeble Hope could ne'er have flown,
But vainly flapped its tinsel wing.

And yet I quickly might arrive
Where my extended soul is fixed,
But Fate does iron wedges drive,
And always crowds itself betwixt.

For Fate with jealous eye does see
Two perfect loves, nor lets them close:
Their union would her ruin be,
And her tyrannic pow'r depose.

And therefore her decrees of steel
Us as the distant poles have placed,
(Though Love's whole world on us doth wheel)
Not by themselves to be embraced,

Unless the giddy heaven fall,
And earth some new convulsion tear;
And, us to join, the world should all
Be cramped into a planisphere.

As lines, so loves oblique may well
Themselves in every angle greet;
But ours so truly parallel,
Though infinite, can never meet.

Therefore the love which us doth bind,
But Fate so enviously debars,
Is the conjunction of the mind,
And opposition of the stars.

MICHEAL O'SIADHAIL

Between

As we fall into step I ask a penny for your thoughts.
'Oh, nothing,' you say, 'well, nothing so easily bought.'

Sliding into the rhythm of your silence, I almost forget
how lonely I'd been until that autumn morning we met.

At bedtime up along my childhood's stairway, tongues
of fire cast shadows. Too earnest, too highstrung.

My desire is endless: others ended when I'd only started.
Then, there was you: so whole-hog, so wholehearted.

Think of the thousands of nights and the shadows fought.
And the mornings of light. I try to read your thought.

In the strange openness of your face, I'm powerless.
Always this love. Always this infinity between us.

JOHN DONNE

Air and Angels

Twice or thrice had I loved thee,
Before I knew thy face or name;
So in a voice, so in a shapeless flame,
Angels affect us oft, and worshipped be.
    Still when, to where thou wert, I came
Some lovely glorious nothing I did see,
    But since my soul, whose child love is,
Takes limbs of flesh, and else could nothing do,
    More subtle than the parent is,
Love must not be, but take a body too,
    And therefore what thou wert, and who,
        I bid love ask; and now
That it assume thy body I allow,
And fix itself in thy lip, eye, and brow.

Whilst thus to ballast love I thought,
And so more steadily to have gone,
With wares which would sink admiration,
I saw I had love's pinnace over-fraught:
    Ev'ry thy hair for love to work upon
Is much too much, some fitter must be sought;
    For, nor in nothing, nor in things
Extreme, and scatt'ring bright, can love inhere;
    Then, as an angel, face and wings
Of air, not pure as it, yet pure doth wear,
    So thy love may be my love's sphere;
        Just such disparity
As is 'twixt air and angels' purity,
'Twixt women's love, and men's will ever be.

LOUIS MACNEICE

Coda

Maybe we knew each other better
When the night was young and unrepeated
And the moon stood still over Jericho.

So much for the past; in the present
There are moments caught between heart-beats
When maybe we know each other better.

But what is that clinking in the darkness?
Maybe we shall know each other better
When the tunnels meet beneath the mountain.

CAROL ANN DUFFY

Words, Wide Night

Somewhere, on the other side of this wide night
and the distance between us, I am thinking of you.
The room is turning slowly away from the moon.

This is pleasurable. Or shall I cross that out and say
it is sad? In one of the tenses I singing
an impossible song of desire that you cannot hear.

La lala la. See? I close my eyes and imagine
the dark hills I would have to cross
to reach you. For I am in love with you and this

is what it is like or what it is like in words.

PHILIP LARKIN

Broadcast

Giant whispering and coughing from
Vast Sunday-full and organ-frowned-on spaces
Precede a sudden scuttle on the drum,
'The Queen', and huge resettling. Then begins
A snivel on the violins:
I think of your face among all those faces,

Beautiful and devout before
Cascades of monumental slithering,
One of your gloves unnoticed on the floor
Beside those new, slightly-outmoded shoes.
Here it goes quickly dark. I lose
All but the outline of the still and withering

Leaves on half-emptied trees. Behind
The glowing wavebands, rabid storms of chording
By being distant overpower my mind
All the more shamelessly, their cut-off shout
Leaving me desperate to pick out
Your hands, tiny in all that air, applauding.

AMY LOWELL

The Letter

Little cramped words scrawling all over the paper
Like draggled fly's legs,
What can you tell of the flaring moon
Through the oak leaves?
Or of my uncurtained window and the bare floor
Spattered with moonlight?
Your silly quirks and twists have nothing in them
Of blossoming hawthorns,
And this paper is dull, crisp, smooth, virgin of loveliness
Beneath my hand.

I am tired, Beloved, of chafing my heart against
The want of you;
Of squeezing it into little inkdrops,
And posting it.
And I scald alone, here, under the fire
Of the great moon.

CHINUA ACHEBE

Love Song (for Anna)

Bear with me my love
in the hour of my silence;
the air is crisscrossed
by loud omens and songbirds
fearing reprisals of middle day
have hidden away their notes
wrapped up in leaves
of cocoyam . . . What song shall I
sing to you my love when
a choir of squatting toads
turns the stomach of day with
goitrous adoration of an infested
swamp and purple-headed
vultures at home stand
sentry on the rooftop?

I will sing only in waiting
silence your power to bear
my dream for me in your quiet
eyes and wrap the dust of our blistered
feet in golden anklets ready
for the return someday of our
banished dance.

The Shortest and Sweetest of Songs

Come
Home.

The Avenue

Who has not seen their lover
Walking at ease,
Walking like any other
A pavement under trees,
Not singular, apart,
But footed, featured, dressed,
Approaching like the rest
In the same dapple of the summer caught;
Who has not suddenly thought
With swift surprise:
There walks in cool disguise,
There comes, my heart?

With a vow

ELIZABETH GARRETT

Epithalamium

Ask not, this night, how we shall love
When we are three-year lovers;
How clothes, as lapsing tides, as love,
May slide, three summers over;
Nor ask when the eye's quick darknesses
Throw shadows on our skin
How we shall know our nakedness
In the difference of things.

Ask not whose salty hand turns back
The sea's sheet on the shore,
Or how the spilt and broken moon rides
Still each wave's humped back –
Ask not, for it is given as my pledge
That night shall be our sole inquisitor,
Day our respondent, and each parting as the bride
And groom, an hour before their marriage.

SIR EDWIN ARNOLD

Destiny

Somewhere there waiteth in this world of ours
For one lone soul another lonely soul,
Each choosing each through all the weary hours
And meeting strangely at one sudden goal.
Then blend they, like green leaves with golden flowers,
Into one beautiful and perfect whole;
And life's long night is ended, and the way
Lies open onward to eternal day.

BRIAN PATTEN

January Gladsong

Seeing as yet nothing is really well enough arranged
the dragonfly will not yet sing
nor will the guests ever arrive
quite as naked as the tulips intended.
Still, because once again I am wholly glad of living,
I will make all that is possible step out of time
to a land of giant hurrays! where the happy monsters dance
and stomp darkness down.

Because joy and sorrow must finally unite and the small heart-
beat of sparrow be heard above jet-roar, I will sing
not of tomorrow's impossible paradise
but of what now radiates.
Forever the wind is blowing the white clouds in someone's
    pure direction.

In all our time birdsong has teemed and couples known
that darkness is not forever.
In the glad boat we sail the gentle and invisible ocean
where none have ever really drowned.

W. H. AUDEN

Carry her over the water,
    And set her down under the tree,
Where the culvers white all day and all night,
    And the winds from every quarter,
Sing agreeably, agreeably, agreeably of love.

Put a gold ring on her finger,
    And press her close to your heart,
While the fish in the lake their snapshots take,
    And the frog, that sanguine singer,
Sings agreeably, agreeably, agreeably of love.

The streets shall all flock to your marriage,
    The houses turn round to look,
The tables and chairs say suitable prayers,
    And the horses drawing your carriage
Sing agreeably, agreeably, agreeably of love.

Even like two little bank-dividing brooks,
   That wash the pebbles with their wanton streams,
And having ranged and searched a thousand nooks,
   Meet both at length in silver-breasted Thames
     Where in a greater current they conjoin:
So I my Best-Beloved's am, so he is mine.

Even so we met; and after long pursuit
   Even so we joined; we both became entire;
No need for either to renew a suit,
   For I was flax and he was flames of fire:
     Our firm united souls did more than twine,
So I my Best-Beloved's am, so he is mine.

If all those glittering monarchs that command
   The servile quarters of this earthly ball
Should tender in exchange their shares of land,
   I would not change my fortunes for them all:
     Their wealth is but a counter to my coin;
The world's but theirs, but my Beloved's mine.

Nay, more: if the fair Thespian ladies all
   Should heap together their diviner treasure,
That treasure should be deemed a price too small
   To buy a minute's lease of half my pleasure.
     'Tis not the sacred wealth of all the Nine
Can buy my heart from him, or his from being mine.

Nor time, nor place, nor chance, nor death can bow
   My least desires unto the least remove;
He's firmly mine by oath, I his by vow;
   He's mine by faith, and I am his by love;
     He's mine by water, I am his by wine;
Thus I my Best-Beloved's am, thus he is mine.

He is my altar, I his holy place;
   I am his guest, and he my living food;
I'm his by penitence, he mine by grace;
   I'm his by purchase, he is mine by blood;
     He's my supporting elm, and I his vine:
Thus I my Best-Beloved's am, thus he is mine.

He gives me wealth, I give him all my vows;
   I give him songs, he gives me length of days;
With wreaths of grace he crowns my conquering
       brows;
   And I his temples with a crown of praise,
     Which he accepts as an everlasting sign,
That I my Best-Beloved's am: that he is mine.

ALICE OSWALD

Wedding

From time to time our love is like a sail
and when the sail begins to alternate
from tack to tack, it's like a swallowtail
and when the swallow flies it's like a coat;
and if the coat is yours, it has a tear
like a wide mouth and when the mouth begins
to draw the wind, it's like a trumpeter
and when the trumpet blows, it blows like millions . . .
and this, my love, when millions come and go
beyond the need of us, is like a trick;
and when the trick begins, it's like a toe
tip-toeing on a rope, which is like luck;
and when the luck begins, it's like a wedding,
which is like love, which is like everything.

ANONYMOUS

I will give my love an apple without e'er a core,
I will give my love a house without e'er a door,
I will give my love a palace wherein she may be,
And she may unlock it without any key.

My head is the apple without e'er a core,
My mind is the house without e'er a door,
My heart is the palace wherein she may be,
And she may unlock it without any key.

LEMN SISSAY

Invisible Kisses

If there was ever one
Whom when you were sleeping
Would wipe your tears
When in dreams you were weeping;
Who would offer you time
When others demand;
Whose love lay more infinite
Than grains of sand.

If there was ever one
To whom you could cry;
Who would gather each tear
And blow it dry;
Who would offer help
On the mountains of time;
Who would stop to let each sunset
Soothe the jaded mind.

If there was ever one
To whom when you run
Will push back the clouds
So you are bathed in sun;
Who would open arms
If you would fall;
Who would show you everything
If you lost it all.

If there was ever one
Who when you achieve
Was there before the dream
And even then believed;
Who would clear the air
When it's full of loss;
Who would count love
Before the cost.

If there was ever one
Who when you are cold
Will summon warm air
For your hands to hold;
Who would make peace
In pouring pain,
Make laughter fall
In falling rain.

If there was ever one
Who can offer you this and more;
Who in keyless rooms
Can open doors;
Who in open doors
Can see open fields
And in open fields
See harvests yield.

Then see only my face
In the reflection of these tides
Through the clear water
Beyond the river side.
All I can send is love
In all that this is
A poem and a necklace
Of invisible kisses.

JAMES FENTON

Hinterhof

Stay near to me and I'll stay near to you –
As near as you are dear to me will do,
    Near as the rainbow to the rain,
    The west wind to the windowpane,
As fire to the hearth, as dawn to dew.

Stay true to me and I'll stay true to you –
As true as you are new to me will do,
    New as the rainbow in the spray,
    Utterly new in every way,
New in the way that what you say is true.

Stay near to me, stay true to me. I'll stay
As near, as true to you as heart could pray.
    Heart never hoped that one might be
    Half of the things you are to me –
The dawn, the fire, the rainbow and the day.

JOSHUA SYLVESTER

Were I as base as is the lowly plain,
And you, my Love, as high as heaven above,
Yet should the thoughts of me your humble swain
Ascend to heaven in honour of my Love.
Were I as high as heaven above the plain,
And you, my Love, as humble and as low
As are the deepest bottoms of the main,
Whereso'er you were, with you my love should go.
Were you the earth, dear Love, and I the skies,
My Love should shine on you like to the sun,
And look upon you with ten thousand eyes,
Till heaven waxed blind, and till the world were done.
Whereso'er I am, below or else above you,
Whereso'er you are, my heart shall truly love you.

E. E. CUMMINGS

i carry your heart with me(i carry it in
my heart)i am never without it(anywhere
i go you go,my dear;and whatever is done
by only me is your doing,my darling)
                                                    i fear
no fate(for you are my fate,my sweet)i want
no world(for beautiful you are my world,my true)
and it's you are whatever a moon has always meant
and whatever a sun will always sing is you

here is the deepest secret nobody knows
(here is the root of the root and the bud of the bud
and the sky of the sky of a tree called life;which grows
higher than soul can hope or mind can hide)
and this is the wonder that's keeping the stars apart

i carry your heart(i carry it in my heart)

GEORGE CHAPMAN

from *The Masque of the Middle Temple and Lincoln's Inn*

Bridal Song

Now, Sleep, bind fast the flood of air,
    Strike all things dumb and deaf,
And to disturb our nuptial pair
    Let stir no aspen leaf.
Send flocks of golden dreams
    That all true joys presage;
Bring, in thy oily streams,
    The milk-and-honey age.
Now close the world-round sphere of bliss,
And fill it with a heavenly kiss.

MICHAEL DONAGHY

The Present

For the present there is just one moon,
though every level pond gives back another.

But the bright disc shining in the black lagoon,
perceived by astrophysicist and lover,

is milliseconds old. And even that light's
seven minutes older than its source.

And the stars we think we see on moonless nights
are long extinguished. And, of course,

this very moment, as you read this line,
is literally gone before you know it.

Forget the here-and-now. We have no time
but this device of wantonness and wit.

Make me this present then: your hand in mine,
and we'll live out our lives in it.

KATE CLANCHY

Patagonia

I said *perhaps Patagonia*, and pictured
a peninsula, wide enough
for a couple of ladderback chairs
to wobble on at high tide. I thought

of us in breathless cold, facing
a horizon round as a coin, looped
in a cat's cradle strung by gulls
from sea to sun. I planned to wait

till the waves had bored themselves
to sleep, till the last clinging barnacles,
growing worried in the hush, had
paddled off in tiny coracles, till

those restless birds, your actor's hands,
had dropped slack into your lap,
until you'd turned, at last, to me.
When I spoke of Patagonia, I meant

skies all empty aching blue. I meant
years. I meant all of them with you.

Happily ever after

C. K. WILLIAMS

Love: Beginnings

They're at that stage where so much desire streams between
    them, so much frank need and want,
so much absorption in the other and the self and the
    self-admiring entity and unity they make –
her mouth so full, breast so lifted, head thrown back so far in her
    laughter at his laughter,
he so solid, planted, oaky, firm, so resonantly factual in the
    headiness of being craved so,
she almost wreathed upon him as they intertwine again, touch
    again, cheek, lip, shoulder, brow,
every glance moving toward the sexual, every glance away
    soaring back in flame into the sexual –
that just to watch them is to feel again that hitching in the groin,
    that filling of the heart,
the old, sore heart, the battered, foundered, faithful heart,
    snorting again, stamping in its stall.

MURIEL RUKEYSER

Looking at Each Other

Yes, we were looking at each other
Yes, we knew each other very well
Yes, we had made love with each other many times
Yes, we had heard music together
Yes, we had gone to the sea together
Yes, we had cooked and eaten together
Yes, we had laughed often day and night
Yes, we fought violence and knew violence
Yes, we hated the inner and outer oppression
Yes, that day we were looking at each other
Yes, we saw the sunlight pouring down
Yes, the corner of the table was between us
Yes, bread and flowers were on the table
Yes, our eyes saw each other's eyes
Yes, our mouths saw each other's mouth
Yes, our breasts saw each other's breasts
Yes, our bodies entire saw each other
Yes, it was beginning in each
Yes, it threw waves across our lives
Yes, the pulses were becoming very strong
Yes, the beating became very delicate
Yes, the calling   the arousal
Yes, the arriving   the coming
Yes, there it was for both entire
Yes, we were looking at each other

TED HUGHES

Bride and Groom Lie Hidden for Three Days

She gives him his eyes, she found them
Among some rubble, among some beetles

He gives her her skin
He just seemed to pull it down out of the air and lay it over her
She weeps with fearfulness and astonishment

She has found his hands for him, and fitted them freshly at the
    wrists
They are amazed at themselves, they go feeling all over her

He has assembled her spine, he cleaned each piece carefully
And sets them in perfect order
A superhuman puzzle but he is inspired
She leans back twisting this way and that, using it and laughing,
    incredulous

Now she has brought his feet, she is connecting them
So that his whole body lights up
And he has fashioned her new hips
With all fittings complete and with newly wound coils, all
    shiningly oiled
He is polishing every part, he himself can hardly believe it

They keep taking each other to the sun, they find they can easily
To test each new thing at each new step

And now she smooths over him the plates of his skull
So that the joints are invisible
And now he connects her throat, her breasts and the pit of her
    stomach
With a single wire

She gives him his teeth, tying their roots to the centrepin of his
    body

He sets the little circlets on her fingertips

She stitches his body here and there with steely purple silk

He oils the delicate cogs of her mouth

She inlays with deep-cut scrolls the nape of his neck

He sinks into place the inside of her thighs

So, gasping with joy, with cries of wonderment
Like two gods of mud
Sprawling in the dirt, but with infinite care

They bring each other to perfection.

WILLIAM BLAKE

When a Man has Married a Wife
    he finds out whether
Her knees & elbows are only
    glued together

215

JOHN MILTON

from *Paradise Lost*, Book IX

Thus Eve with count'nance blithe her story told;
But in her cheek distemper flushing glowed.
On th' other side, Adam, soon as he heard
The fatal trespass done by Eve, amazed,
Astonied stood and blank, while horror chill
Ran through his veins, and all his joints relaxed;
From his slack hand the garland wreathed for Eve
Down dropped, and all the faded roses shed:
Speechless he stood and pale, till thus at length
First to himself he inward silence broke.
    O fairest of Creation, last and best
Of all God's works, creature in whom excelled
Whatever can to sight or thought be formed,
Holy, divine, good, amiable or sweet!
How art thou lost, how on a sudden lost,
Defaced, deflow'red, and now to death devote?
Rather how hast thou yielded to transgress
The strict forbiddance, how to violate
The sacred fruit forbidd'n! Some cursèd fraud
Of Enemy hath beguiled thee, yet unknown,
And me with thee hath ruined, for with thee
Certain my resolution is to die;
How can I live without thee, how forgo
Thy sweet convérse and love so dearly joined,
To live again in these wild woods forlorn?
Should God create another Eve, and I
Another rib afford, yet loss of thee
Would never from my heart; no no, I feel
The link of nature draw me: flesh of flesh,
Bone of my bone thou art, and from thy state
Mine never shall be parted, bliss or woe.

ALDEN NOWLAN

Parlour Game

We were sitting there
hating one another when
some friends dropped in
who've always said
we're the most loving
couple they know

and of course the two of us
went into the act
as usual, each afraid
of the other's equally
strong inclination
to give the game away,

both sneering inwardly
for the first five or ten
minutes and then
both trying not to burst,
without knowing whether
the laughter that came
would be savage or joyous

– and within half an hour
we caught ourselves exchanging
silly and affectionate
smiles even when
nobody else was watching:

for the millionth time,
starting over again.

WILLIAM BARNES

Jeäne

We now mid hope vor better cheer,
My smilen wife o' twice vive year.
Let others frown, if thou bist near
    Wi' hope upon thy brow, Jeäne;
Vor I vu'st lov'd thee when thy light
Young sheäpe vu'st grew to woman's height;
I loved thee near, an' out o' zight,
    An' I do love thee now, Jeäne.

An' we've a-trod the sheenen bleäde
Ov eegrass in the zummer sheäde,
An' when the leäves begun to feäde
    Wi' zummer in the weäne, Jeäne;
An' we've a-wander'd drough the groun'
O' swaÿen wheat a-turnen brown,
An' we've a-stroll'd together roun'
    The brook an' drough the leäne, Jeäne.

An' nwone but I can ever tell
Ov all thy tears that have a-vell
When trials meäde thy bosom zwell,
    An' nwone but thou o' mine, Jeäne;
An' now my heart, that heav'd wi' pride
Back then to have thee at my zide,
Do love thee mwore as years do slide,
    An' leäve them times behine, Jeäne.

SEAMUS HEANEY

Scaffolding

Masons, when they start upon a building,
Are careful to test out the scaffolding;

Make sure that planks won't slip at busy points,
Secure all ladders, tighten bolted joints.

And yet all this comes down when the job's done
Showing off walls of sure and solid stone.

So if, my dear, there sometimes seem to be
Old bridges breaking between you and me

Never fear. We may let the scaffolds fall
Confident that we have built our wall.

U. A. FANTHORPE

Atlas

There is a kind of love called maintenance,
Which stores the WD40 and knows when to use it;

Which checks the insurance, and doesn't forget
The milkman; which remembers to plant bulbs;

Which answers letters; which knows the way
The money goes; which deals with dentists

And Road Fund Tax and meeting trains,
And postcards to the lonely; which upholds

The permanently ricketty elaborate
Structures of living; which is Atlas.

And maintenance is the sensible side of love,
Which knows what time and weather are doing
To my brickwork; insulates my faulty wiring;
Laughs at my dryrotten jokes; remembers
My need for gloss and grouting; which keeps
My suspect edifice upright in air,
As Atlas did the sky.

PHYLLIS MCGINLEY

The 5:32

She said, If tomorrow my world were torn in two,
Blacked out, dissolved, I think I would remember
(As if transfixed in unsurrendering amber)
This hour best of all the hours I knew:
When cars came backing into the shabby station,
Children scuffing the seats, and the women driving
With ribbons around their hair, and the trains arriving,
And the men getting off with tired but practiced motion.

Yes, I would remember my life this, she said:
Autumn, the platform red with Virginia creeper,
And a man coming toward me, smiling, the evening paper
Under his arm, and his hat pushed back on his head;
And wood smoke lying like haze on the quiet town,
And dinner waiting, and the sun not yet gone down.

SHARON OLDS

True Love

In the middle of the night, when we get up
after making love, we look at each other in
complete friendship, we know so fully
what the other has been doing. Bound to each other
like mountaineers coming down from a mountain,
bound with the tie of the delivery-room,
we wander down the hall to the bathroom, I can
hardly walk, I wobble through the granular
shadowless air, I know where you are
with my eyes closed, we are bound to each other
with huge invisible threads, our sexes
muted, exhausted, crushed, the whole
body a sex – surely this
is the most blessed time of my life,
our children asleep in their beds, each fate
like a vein of abiding mineral
not discovered yet. I sit
on the toilet in the night, you are somewhere in the room,
I open the window and snow has fallen in a
steep drift, against the pane, I
look up, into it,
a wall of cold crystals, silent
and glistening, I quietly call to you
and you come and hold my hand and I say
I cannot see beyond it. I cannot see beyond it.

RICHARD WILBUR

For C.

After the clash of elevator gates
And the long sinking, she emerges where,
A slight thing in the morning's crosstown glare,
She looks up toward the window where he waits,
Then in a fleeting taxi joins the rest
Of the huge traffic bound forever west.

On such grand scale do lovers say good-bye –
Even this other pair whose high romance
Had only the duration of a dance,
And who, now taking leave with stricken eye,
See each in each a whole new life forgone.
For them, above the darkling clubhouse lawn,

Bright Perseids flash and crumble; while for these
Who part now on the dock, weighed down by grief
And baggage, yet with something like relief,
It takes three thousand miles of knitting seas
To cancel out their crossing, and unmake
The amorous rough and tumble of their wake.

We are denied, my love, their fine tristesse
And bittersweet regrets, and cannot share
The frequent vistas of their large despair,
Where love and all are swept to nothingness;
Still, there's a certain scope in that long love
Which constant spirits are the keepers of,

And which, though taken to be tame and staid,
Is a wild sostenuto of the heart,
A passion joined to courtesy and art
Which has the quality of something made,
Like a good fiddle, like the rose's scent,
Like a rose window or the firmament.

JOHN KEATS

Bright star! would I were steadfast as thou art –
   Not in lone splendour hung aloft the night
And watching, with eternal lids apart,
   Like nature's patient, sleepless Eremite,
The moving waters at their priestlike task
   Of pure ablution round earth's human shores,
Or gazing on the new soft-fallen mask
   Of snow upon the mountains and the moors –
No – yet still steadfast, still unchangeable,
   Pillowed upon my fair love's ripening breast,
To feel for ever its soft swell and fall,
   Awake for ever in a sweet unrest,
Still, still to hear her tender-taken breath,
And so live ever – or else swoon to death.

Treacherously

THOMAS MOORE

On Taking a Wife

'Come, come,' said Tom's father, 'at your time of life,
  There's no longer excuse for thus playing the rake.
It's time you should think, boy, of taking a wife.'
  'Why so it is, father. Whose wife shall I take?'

may i feel said he
(i'll squeal said she
just once said he)
it's fun said she

(may i touch said he
how much said she
a lot said he)
why not said she

(let's go said he
not too far said she
what's too far said he
where you are said she)

may i stay said he
(which way said she
like this said he
if you kiss said she

may i move said he
is it love said she)
if you're willing said he
(but you're killing said she

but it's life said he
but your wife said she
now said he)
ow said she

(tiptop said he
don't stop said she
oh no said he)
go slow said she

(cccome?said he
ummm said she)
you're divine!said he
(you are Mine said she)

ISOBEL DIXON

You, Me and the Orang-utan

Forgive me, it was not my plan
to fall in love like this. You are the best of men,
but he is something else. A king
among the puny; gentle, nurturing.

Walking without you through the zoo, I felt his gaze,
love at first sight, yes, but through the bars, alas.
Believe me, though, it's not a question of his size –
what did it for me were his supple lips, those melancholy eyes,

that noble, furrowed brow. His heart, so filled with care
for every species. And his own, so threatened, rare –
how could I not respond, there are so few like him these days?
Don't try to ape him or dissuade me, darling, please.

For now I think of little else, although
it's hopeless and it can't go on, I know –
I lie here, burning, on our bed, and think of Borneo.

GEORGE GORDON, LORD BYRON

from *Don Juan*, Canto I

CXXXVI

'Twas midnight – Donna Julia was in bed,
  Sleeping, most probably, – when at her door
Arose a clatter might awake the dead,
  If they had never been awoke before,
And that they have been so we all have read,
  And are to be so, at the least, once more –
The door was fasten'd, but with voice and fist
First knocks were heard, then 'Madam – Madam – hist!'

CXXXVII

'For God's sake, Madam – Madam – here's my master,
  With more than half the city at his back –
Was ever heard of such a curst disaster!
  'Tis not my fault – I kept good watch – Alack!
Do, pray undo the bolt a little faster –
  They're on the stair just now, and in a crack
Will all be here; perhaps he yet may fly –
Surely the window's not so *very* high!'

CXXXVIII

By this time Don Alfonso was arrived,
  With torches, friends, and servants in great number;
The major part of them had long been wived,
  And therefore paused not to disturb the slumber
Of any wicked woman, who contrived
  By stealth her husband's temples to encumber:
Examples of this kind are so contagious,
Were *one* not punish'd, *all* would be outrageous.

I can't tell how, or why, or what suspicion
   Could enter into Don Alfonso's head;
But for a cavalier of his condition
   It surely was exceedingly ill-bred,
Without a word of previous admonition,
   To hold a levee round his lady's bed,
And summon lackeys, arm'd with fire and sword,
To prove himself the thing he most abhorr'd.

Poor Donna Julia! starting as from sleep,
   (Mind – that I do not say – she had not slept)
Began at once to scream, and yawn, and weep;
   Her maid Antonia, who was an adept,
Contrived to fling the bed-clothes in a heap,
   As if she had just now from out them crept:
I can't tell why she should take all this trouble
To prove her mistress had been sleeping double.

But Julia mistress, and Antonia maid,
   Appear'd like two poor harmless women, who
Of goblins, but still more of men afraid,
   Had thought one man might be deterr'd by two,
And therefore side by side were gently laid,
   Until the hours of absence should run through,
And truant husband should return, and say,
'My dear, I was the first who came away.'

Now Julia found at length a voice, and cried,
   'In heaven's name, Don Alfonso, what d'ye mean?
Has madness seized you? would that I had died
   Ere such a monster's victim I had been!
What may this midnight violence betide,
   A sudden fit of drunkenness or spleen?
Dare you suspect me, whom the thought would kill?
Search, then, the room!' – Alfonso said, 'I will.'

He search'd, *they* search'd, and rummaged every where,
    Closet and clothes'-press, chest and window-seat,
And found much linen, lace, and several pair
    Of stockings, slippers, brushes, combs, complete,
With other articles of ladies fair,
    To keep them beautiful, or leave them neat:
Arras they prick'd and curtains with their swords,
And wounded several shutters, and some boards.

Under the bed they search'd, and there they found –
    No matter what – it was not that they sought;
They open'd windows, gazing if the ground
    Had signs or footmarks, but the earth said nought;
And then they stared each other's faces round:
    'Tis odd, not one of all these seekers thought,
And seems to me almost a sort of blunder,
Of looking *in* the bed as well as under.

MARY COLERIDGE

Jealousy

'The myrtle bush grew shady
    Down by the ford.' –
'Is it even so?' said my lady.
    'Even so!' said my lord.
'The leaves are set too thick together
    For the point of a sword.'

'The arras in your room hangs close,
    No light between!
You wedded one of those
    That see unseen.' –
'Is it even so?' said the King's Majesty.
    'Even so!' said the Queen.

EDWARD ARLINGTON ROBINSON

Firelight

Ten years together without yet a cloud,
They seek each other's eyes at intervals
Of gratefulness to firelight and four walls
For love's obliteration of the crowd.
Serenely and perennially endowed
And bowered as few may be, their joy recalls
No snake, no sword; and over them there falls
The blessing of what neither says aloud.

Wiser for silence, they were not so glad
Were she to read the graven tale of lines
On the wan face of one somewhere alone;
Nor were they more content could he have had
Her thoughts a moment since of one who shines
Apart, and would be hers if he had known.

ADAM O'RIORDAN

Cheat

As in the beach scene framed on this postcard,
where a jovial uncle is packed into sand
until even his head disappears below ground.
Just so, Ovid tells how unchaste Vestal Virgins
were shovelled under, quite alive but drowsy,
no longer afraid of the dark or the weight
of the dirt that will drown them.

In this dingy pub, cinders in a grate dust over.
I dab the tip of my nose for your odour,
remembering how, like a pontiff wet with balm,
when anointing, I sunk with the fluke of your hips,
our movements incessant as a distaff and spindle.
Then, with him away and your place empty,
how we changed, stepped up our game and conjured:

two mongrel dogs locked and hot with instinct,
became a horse the rider moves in time with.
Our spent bodies: eels fetched up in a bucket.
Night reclaims the light, a bell chimes,
my glass is drained; through the window pane
this interior steadies itself on the street.
I watch the stream of passers-by walk through me.

LAVINIA GREENLAW

Tryst

Night slips, trailing behind it
a suddenly innocent darkness.
Am I safe, now, to slip home?

My fists tighten your collar, your fingers
lock in my hair and we hover
between discretion and advertised purpose.

Dawn traffic in both directions,
taxis, milk floats, builders' vans.
Each proposes a service or poses a threat

like the police, slumped couples in cars
left to patrol each other, to converge
at a red light that stops little else.

Each separation is outweighed
by more faith, more sadness;
accumulated static, the shock in every step.

I go to sleep where my life is sleeping
and wake late to a fused morning,
a blistered mouth.

JULIA COPUS

In Defence of Adultery

We don't fall in love: it rises through us
the way that certain music does –
whether a symphony or ballad –
and it is sepia-coloured,
like spilt tea that inches up
the tiny tube-like gaps inside
a cube of sugar lying by a cup.
Yes, love's like that: just when we least
needed or expected it
a part of us dips into it
by chance or mishap and it seeps
through our capillaries, it clings
inside the chambers of the heart.
We're victims, we say: mere vessels,
drinking the vanilla scent
of this one's skin, the lustre
of another's eyes so skilfully
darkened with bistre. And whatever
damage might result we're not
to blame for it: love is an autocrat
and won't be disobeyed.
Sometimes we manage
to convince ourselves of that.

Brutally

EMILY DICKINSON

He fumbles at your Soul
As Players at the Keys –
Before they drop full Music on –
He stuns you by Degrees –

Prepares your brittle nature
For the etherial Blow
By fainter Hammers – further heard –
Then nearer – Then so – slow –

Your Breath – has time to straighten –
Your Brain – to bubble cool –
Deals One – imperial Thunderbolt –
That scalps your naked soul –

When Winds hold Forests in their Paws –
The Universe – is still –

GEORGE MEREDITH

from *Modern Love*

IX

He felt the wild beast in him betweenwhiles
So masterfully rude, that he would grieve
To see the helpless delicate thing receive
His guardianship through certain dark defiles.
Had he not teeth to rend, and hunger too?
But still he spared her. Once: 'Have you no fear?'
He said: 'twas dusk; she in his grasp; none near.
She laughed: 'No, surely; am I not with you?'
And uttering that soft starry 'you,' she leaned
Her gentle body near him, looking up;
And from her eyes, as from a poison-cup,
He drank until the flittering eyelids screened.
Devilish malignant witch! and oh, young beam
Of heaven's circle-glory! Here thy shape
To squeeze like an intoxicating grape –
I might, and yet thou goest safe, supreme.

AMY LOWELL

Carrefour

O you,
Who came upon me once
Stretched under apple-trees just after bathing,
Why did you not strangle me before speaking
Rather than fill me with the wild white honey of your words
And then leave me to the mercy
Of the forest bees?

WILLIAM SHAKESPEARE
from *Venus and Adonis*

The honey fee of parting tendered is:
  Her arms do lend his neck a sweet embrace;
  Incorporate then they seem; face grows to face.

Till breathless he disjoined, and backward drew
The heavenly moisture, that sweet coral mouth,
Whose precious taste her thirsty lips well knew,
Whereon they surfeit, yet complain on drouth.
  He with her plenty pressed, she faint with dearth,
  Their lips together glued, fall to the earth.

Now quick desire hath caught the yielding prey,
And glutton-like she feeds, yet never filleth;
Her lips are conquerors, his lips obey,
Paying what ransom the insulter willeth;
  Whose vulture thought doth pitch the price so high
  That she will draw his lips' rich treasure dry.

And having felt the sweetness of the spoil,
With blindfold fury she begins to forage;
Her face doth reek and smoke, her blood doth boil,
And careless lust stirs up a desperate courage,
  Planting oblivion, beating reason back,
  Forgetting shame's pure blush and honour's wrack.

Hot, faint and weary, with her hard embracing,
Like a wild bird being tamed with too much handling,
Or as the fleet-foot roe that's tired with chasing,
Or like the froward infant stilled with dandling,
  He now obeys and now no more resisteth,
  While she takes all she can, not all she listeth.

What wax so frozen but dissolves with temp'ring,
And yields at last to every light impression?
Things out of hope are compassed oft with vent'ring,
Chiefly in love, whose leave exceeds commission:
   Affection faints not like a pale-faced coward,
   But then woos best when most his choice is froward.

When he did frown, O, had she then gave over,
Such nectar from his lips she had not sucked.
Foul words and frowns must not repel a lover;
What though the rose have prickles, yet 'tis plucked.
   Were beauty under twenty locks kept fast,
   Yet love breaks through, and picks them all at last.

ALEXANDER POPE

from *The Rape of the Lock*, Canto III

But when to mischief mortals bend their will,
How soon they find fit instruments of ill?
Just then, Clarissa drew with tempting grace
A two-edg'd weapon from her shining case:
So Ladies in Romance assist their Knight,
Present the spear, and arm him for the fight.
He takes the gift with rev'rence, and extends
The little engine on his finger's ends;
This just behind Belinda's neck he spread,
As o'er the fragrant steams she bends her head.
Swift to the Lock a thousand Sprites repair,
A thousand wings, by turns, blow back the hair;
And thrice they twitch'd the diamond in her ear;
Thrice she look'd back, and thrice the foe drew near.
Just in that instant, anxious Ariel sought
The close recesses of the Virgin's thought;
As on the nosegay in her breast reclin'd,
He watch'd th' Ideas rising in her mind,
Sudden he view'd, in spite of all her art,
An earthly Lover lurking at her heart.
Amaz'd, confus'd, he found his pow'r expir'd,
Resign'd to fate, and with a sigh retir'd.
    The Peer now spreads the glitt'ring Forfex wide,
T' inclose the Lock; now joins it, to divide.
Ev'n then, before the fatal engine clos'd,
A wretched Sylph too fondly interpos'd;
Fate urg'd the sheers, and cut the Sylph in twain,
(But airy substance soon unites again)
The meeting points the sacred hair dissever
From the fair head, for ever, and for ever!
    Then flash'd the living lightning from her eyes,
And screams of horror rend th' affrighted skies.

Not louder shrieks to pitying heav'n are cast,
When husbands, or when lapdogs breathe their last,
Or when rich China vessels, fall'n from high,
In glitt'ring dust, and painted fragments lie!
  Let wreaths of triumph now my temples twine,
(The Victor cry'd) the glorious Prize is mine!
While fish in streams, or birds delight in air,
Or in a coach and six the British Fair,
As long as Atalantis shall be read,
Or the small pillow grace a Lady's bed,
While visits shall be paid on solemn days,
When num'rous wax-lights in bright order blaze,
While nymphs take treats, or assignations give,
So long my honour, name, and praise shall live!
What Time would spare, from steel receives its date,
And monuments, like men, submit to fate!
Steel could the labour of the Gods destroy,
And strike to dust th' imperial tow'rs of Troy;
Steel could the works of mortal pride confound,
And hew triumphal arches to the ground.
What wonder then, fair nymph! thy hairs should feel
The conqu'ring force of unresisted steel?

W. B. YEATS

Leda and the Swan

A sudden blow: the great wings beating still
Above the staggering girl, her thighs caressed
By the dark webs, her nape caught in his bill,
He holds her helpless breast upon his breast.

How can those terrified vague fingers push
The feathered glory from her loosening thighs?
And how can body, laid in that white rush,
But feel the strange heart beating where it lies?

A shudder in the loins engenders there
The broken wall, the burning roof and tower
And Agamemnon dead.
                  Being so caught up,
So mastered by the brute blood of the air,
Did she put on his knowledge with his power
Before the indifferent beak could let her drop?

D. H. LAWRENCE

Love on the Farm

What large, dark hands are those at the window
Grasping in the golden light
Which weaves its way through the evening wind
  At my heart's delight?

Ah, only the leaves! But in the west
I see a redness suddenly come
Into the evening's anxious breast –
  'Tis the wound of love goes home!

The woodbine creeps abroad
Calling low to her lover:
  The sun-lit flirt who all the day
  Has poised above her lips in play
  And stolen kisses, shallow and gay
  Of pollen, now has gone away –
   She woos the moth with her sweet, low word:
And when above her his moth-wings hover
Then her bright breast she will uncover
And yield her honey-drop to her lover.

Into the yellow, evening glow
Saunters a man from the farm below;
Leans, and looks in at the low-built shed
Where the swallow has hung her marriage bed.
  The bird lies warm against the wall.
  She glances quick her startled eyes
  Towards him, then she turns away
  Her small head, making warm display
  Of red upon the throat. Her terrors sway
  Her out of the nest's warm, busy ball,
  Whose plaintive cry is heard as she flies
  In one blue stoop from out the sties
  Into the twilight's empty hall.

Oh, water-hen, beside the rushes
Hide your quaintly scarlet blushes,
Still your quick tail, lie still as dead,
Till the distance folds over his ominous tread!

The rabbit presses back her ears,
Turns back her liquid, anguished eyes
And crouches low; then with wild spring
Spurts from the terror of *his* oncoming;
To be choked back, the wire ring
Her frantic effort throttling:
   Piteous brown ball of quivering fears!
Ah, soon in his large, hard hands she dies,
And swings all loose from the swing of his walk!
Yet calm and kindly are his eyes
And ready to open in brown surprise
Should I not answer to his talk
Or should he my tears surmise.

I hear his hand on the latch, and rise from my chair
Watching the door open; he flashes bare
His strong teeth in a smile, and flashes his eyes
In a smile like triumph upon me; then careless-wise
He flings the rabbit soft on the table board
And comes towards me: ah! the uplifted sword
Of his hand against my bosom! and oh, the broad
Blade of his glance that asks me to applaud
His coming! With his hand he turns my face to him
And caresses me with his fingers that still smell grim
Of the rabbit's fur! God, I am caught in a snare!
I know not what fine wire is round my throat;
I only know I let him finger there
My pulse of life, and let him nose like a stoat
Who sniffs with joy before he drinks the blood.

And down his mouth comes to my mouth! and down
His bright dark eyes come over me, like a hood
Upon my mind! his lips meet mine, and a flood
Of sweet fire sweeps across me, so I drown
Against him, die, and find death good.

246

TED HUGHES

Lovesong

He loved her and she loved him
His kisses sucked out her whole past and future or tried to
He had no other appetite
She bit him she gnawed him she sucked
She wanted him complete inside her
Safe and sure forever and ever
Their little cries fluttered into the curtains

Her eyes wanted nothing to get away
Her looks nailed down his hands his wrists his elbows
He gripped her hard so that life
Should not drag her from that moment
He wanted all future to cease
He wanted to topple with his arms round her
Off that moment's brink and into nothing
Or everlasting or whatever there was
Her embrace was an immense press
To print him into her bones
His smiles were the garrets of a fairy palace
Where the real world would never come
Her smiles were spider bites
So he would lie still till she felt hungry
His words were occupying armies
Her laughs were an assassin's attempts
His looks were bullets daggers of revenge
Her glances were ghosts in the corner with horrible secrets
His whispers were whips and jackboots
Her kisses were lawyers steadily writing
His caresses were the last hooks of a castaway
Her love-tricks were the grinding of locks
And their deep cries crawled over the floors
Like an animal dragging a great trap

His promises were the surgeon's gag
Her promises took the top off his skull
She would get a brooch made of it
His vows pulled out all her sinews
He showed her how to make a love-knot
Her vows put his eyes in formalin
At the back of her secret drawer
Their screams stuck in the wall

Their heads fell apart into sleep like the two halves
Of a lopped melon, but love is hard to stop

In their entwined sleep they exchanged arms and legs
In their dreams their brains took each other hostage

In the morning they wore each other's face

ISOBEL DIXON

Truce

You bear the hatchet.
I'll bury my heart.

Bitterly

THOMAS MOORE

To ——

When I loved you, I can't but allow
   I had many an exquisite minute;
But the scorn that I feel for you now
   Hath even more luxury in it!

Thus, whether we're on or we're off,
   Some witchery seems to await you;
To love you is pleasant enough,
   And, oh! 'tis delicious to hate you!

GAVIN EWART

Ending

The love we thought would never stop
now cools like a congealing chop.
The kisses that were hot as curry
are bird-pecks taken in a hurry.
The hands that held electric charges
now lie inert as four moored barges.
The feet that ran to meet a date
are running slow and running late.
The eyes that shone and seldom shut
are victims of a power cut.
The parts that then transmitted joy
are now reserved and cold and coy.
Romance, expected once to stay,
has left a note saying GONE AWAY.

ROSEMARY TONKS

Orpheus in Soho

His search is desperate!
And the little night-shops of the Underworld
With their kiosks ... they know it,
The little bars as full of dust as a stale cake,
None of these places would exist without Orpheus
And how well they know it.

... when the word goes ahead to the next city,
An underworld is hastily constructed,
With bitch-clubs, with cellars and passages,
So that he can go on searching, desperately!

As the brim of the world is lit,
And breath pours softly over the Earth,
And as Heaven moves ahead to the next city
With deep airs, and with lights and rains,

He plunges into Hades, for his search is desperate!
And there is so little risk ... down there,
That is the benefit of searching frenziedly
Among the dust-shops and blind-alleys
... there is so little risk of finding her
In Europe's old blue Kasbah, and he knows it.

BABETTE DEUTSCH

Solitude

There is the loneliness of peopled places:
Streets roaring with their human flood; the crowd
That fills bright rooms with billowing sounds and faces,
Like foreign music, overshrill and loud.
There is the loneliness of one who stands
Fronting the waste under the cold sea-light,
A wisp of flesh against the endless sands,
Like a lost gull in solitary flight.
Single is all up-rising and down-lying;
Struggle or fear or silence none may share;
Each is alone in bearing and in dying;
Conquest is uncompanioned as despair.
Yet I have known no loneliness like this,
Locked in your arms and bent beneath your kiss.

When the lamp is shattered
The light in the dust lies dead –
  When the cloud is scattered
The rainbow's glory is shed.
  When the lute is broken,
Sweet tones are remembered not;
  When the lips have spoken,
Loved accents are soon forgot.

  As music and splendour
Survive not the lamp and the lute,
  The heart's echoes render
No song when the spirit is mute:–
  No song but sad dirges,
Like the wind through a ruined cell,
  Or the mournful surges
That ring the dead seaman's knell.

  When hearts have once mingled
Love first leaves the well-built nest;
  The weak one is singled
To endure what it once possessed.
  O Love! who bewailest
The frailty of all things here,
  Why choose you the frailest
For your cradle, your home, and your bier?

  Its passions will rock thee
As the storms rock the ravens on high;
  Bright reason will mock thee,
Like the sun from a wintry sky.
  From thy nest every rafter
Will rot, and thine eagle home
  Leave thee naked to laughter,
When leaves fall and cold winds come.

THOMAS HARDY

Neutral Tones

We stood by a pond that winter day,
And the sun was white, as though chidden of God,
And a few leaves lay on the starving sod;
    – They had fallen from an ash, and were gray.

Your eyes on me were as eyes that rove
Over tedious riddles of years ago;
And some words played between us to and fro
    On which lost the more by our love.

The smile on your mouth was the deadest thing
Alive enough to have strength to die;
And a grin of bitterness swept thereby
    Like an ominous bird a-wing . . .

Since then, keen lessons that love deceives,
And wrings with wrong, have shaped to me
Your face, and the God-curst sun, and a tree,
    And a pond edged with grayish leaves.

CHARLOTTE MEW

Rooms

I remember rooms that have had their part
In the steady slowing down of the heart;
The room in Paris, the room at Geneva,
The little damp room with the seaweed smell
And that ceaseless maddening sound of the tide –
 Rooms where for good or for ill, things died:
But there is the room where we two lie dead
Though every morning we seem to wake, and might just as
  well seem to sleep again
 As we shall some day in the other dustier quieter bed
 Out there – in the sun – in the rain.

The Other Two

All summer we moved in a villa brimful of echoes,
Cool as the pearled interior of a conch.
Bells, hooves, of the high-stepping black goats woke us.
Around our bed the baronial furniture
Foundered through levels of light seagreen and strange.
Not one leaf wrinkled in the clearing air.
We dreamed how we were perfect, and we were.

Against bare, whitewashed walls, the furniture
Anchored itself, griffin-legged and darkly grained.
Two of us in a place meant for ten more –
Our footsteps multiplied in the shadowy chambers,
Our voices fathomed a profounder sound:
The walnut banquet table, the twelve chairs
Mirrored the intricate gestures of two others.

Heavy as statuary, shapes not ours
Performed a dumbshow in the polished wood,
That cabinet without windows or doors:
He lifts an arm to bring her close, but she
Shies from his touch: his is an iron mood.
Seeing her freeze, he turns his face away.
They poise and grieve as in some old tragedy.

Moon-blanched and implacable, he and she
Would not be eased, released. Our each example
Of tenderness dove through their purgatory
Like a planet, a stone, swallowed in a great darkness,
Leaving no sparky track, setting up no ripple.
Nightly we left them in their desert place.
Lights out, they dogged us, sleepless and envious:

We dreamed their arguments, their stricken voices.
We might embrace, but those two never did,
Come, so unlike us, to a stiff impasse,
Burdened in such a way we seemed the lighter –
Ourselves the haunters, and they, flesh and blood;
As if, above love's ruinage, we were
The heaven those two dreamed of, in despair.

GEORGE MEREDITH

from *Modern Love*

I

By this he knew she wept with waking eyes:
That, at his hand's light quiver by her head,
The strange low sobs that shook their common bed,
Were called into her with a sharp surprise,
And strangled mute, like little gaping snakes,
Dreadfully venomous to him. She lay
Stone-still, and the long darkness flowed away
With muffled pulses. Then, as midnight makes
Her giant heart of Memory and Tears
Drink the pale drug of silence, and so beat
Sleep's heavy measure, they from head to feet
Were moveless, looking through their dead black years,
By vain regret scrawled over the blank wall.
Like sculptured effigies they might be seen
Upon their marriage-tomb, the sword between;
Each wishing for the sword that severs all.

DON PATERSON

The Wreck

But what lovers we were, what lovers,
even when it was all over –

the deadweight, bull-black wines we swung
towards each other rang and rang

like bells of blood, our own great hearts.
We slung the drunk boat out of port

and watched our unreal sober life
unmoor, a continent of grief;

the candlelight strange on our faces
like the tiny silent blazes

and coruscations of its wars.
We blew them out and took the stairs

into the night for the night's work,
stripped off in the timbered dark,

gently hooked each other on
like aqualungs, and thundered down

to mine our lovely secret wreck.
We surfaced later, breathless, back

to back, then made our way alone
up the mined beach of the dawn.

In the desert
I saw a creature, naked, bestial,
Who, squatting upon the ground,
Held his heart in his hands,
And ate of it.
I said, 'Is it good, friend?'
'It is bitter – bitter,' he answered;
'But I like it
Because it is bitter,
And because it is my heart.'

Finally

EMILY DICKINSON

My life closed twice before its close –
It yet remains to see
If Immortality unveil
A third event to me

So huge, so hopeless to conceive
As these that twice befell.
Parting is all we know of heaven,
And all we need of hell.

THOMAS HARDY

In the Vaulted Way

In the vaulted way, where the passage turned
To the shadowy corner that none could see,
You paused for our parting, – plaintively;
Though overnight had come words that burned
My fond frail happiness out of me.

And then I kissed you, – despite my thought
That our spell must end when reflection came
On what you had deemed me, whose one long aim
Had been to serve you; that what I sought
Lay not in a heart that could breathe such blame.

But yet I kissed you; whereon you again
As of old kissed me. Why, why was it so?
Do you cleave to me after that light-tongued blow?
If you scorned me at eventide, how love then?
The thing is dark, Dear. I do not know.

KATHERINE MANSFIELD

The Meeting

We started speaking –
Looked at each other; then turned away –
The tears kept rising to my eyes
But I could not weep
I wanted to take your hand
But my hand trembled.
You kept counting the days
Before we should meet again
But both of us felt in our heart
That we parted for ever and ever.
The ticking of the little clock filled the quiet room –
Listen I said; it is so loud
Like a horse galloping on a lonely road.
As loud as that – a horse galloping past in the night.
You shut me up in your arms –
But the sound of the clock stifled our hearts' beating.

You said 'I cannot go: all that is living of me
Is here for ever and ever.'
Then you went.
The world changed. The sound of the clock grew fainter
Dwindled away – became a minute thing –
I whispered in the darkness: 'If it stops, I shall die.'

JENNY JOSEPH

Dawn walkers

Anxious eyes loom down the damp-black streets
Pale staring girls who are walking away hard
From beds where love went wrong or died or turned away,
Treading their misery beneath another day
Stamping to work into another morning.

In all our youths there must have been some time
When the cold dark has stiffened up the wind
But suddenly, like a sail stiffening with wind,
Carried the vessel on, stretching the ropes, glad of it.

But listen to this now: this I saw one morning.
I saw a young man running, for a bus I thought,
Needing to catch it on this murky morning
Dodging the people crowding to work or shopping early.
And all heads stopped and turned to see how he ran
To see would he make it, the beautiful strong young man.
Then I noticed a girl running after, calling out 'John'.
He must have left his sandwiches I thought.
But she screamed 'John wait'. He heard her and ran faster,
Using his muscled legs and studded boots.
We knew she'd never reach him. 'Listen to me John.
Only once more' she cried. 'For the last time, John, please wait,
    please listen.'
He gained the corner in a spurt and she
Sobbing and hopping with her red hair loose
(Made way for by the respectful audience)
Followed on after, but not to catch him now.
Only that there was nothing left to do.

The street closed in and went on with its day.
A worn old man standing in the heat from the baker's
Said 'Surely to God the bastard could have waited.'

HENRY KING
The Surrender

My once dear Love! hapless that I no more
Must call thee so; the rich affection's store
That fed our hopes, lies now exhaust and spent,
Like sums of treasure unto bankrupts lent.

We, that did nothing study but the way
To love each other, with which thoughts the day
Rose with delight to us, and with them, set,
Must learn the hateful art, how to forget.

We, that did nothing wish that Heav'n could give,
Beyond ourselves, nor did desire to live
Beyond that wish, all these now cancel must,
As if not writ in faith, but words and dust.

Yet witness those clear vows which lovers make,
Witness the chaste desires that never brake
Into unruly heats; witness that breast
Which in thy bosom anchor'd his whole rest,
'Tis no default in us; I dare acquite
Thy maiden faith, thy purpose fair and white,
As thy pure self. Cross planets did envy
Us to each other, and Heaven did untie
Faster than vows could bind. O that the stars,
When lovers meet, should stand oppos'd in wars!

Since then some higher Destinies command,
Let us not strive nor labour to withstand
What is past help. The longest date of grief
Can never yield a hope of our relief;
And though we waste ourselves in moist laments,
Tears may drown us, but not our discontents.

Fold back our arms, take home our fruitless loves,
That must new fortunes try, like turtle-doves
Dislodged from their haunts. We must in tears
Unwind a love knit up in many years.
In this last kiss I here surrender thee
Back to thyself, so thou again art free.
Thou in another, sad as that, resend
The truest heart that lover ere did lend.

Now turn from each. So fare our sever'd hearts,
As the divorc'd soul from her body parts.

JOHN DONNE

The Expiration

So, so, break off this last lamenting kiss,
    Which sucks two souls, and vapours both away,
Turn thou ghost that way, and let me turn this,
    And let ourselves benight our happiest day,
We asked none leave to love; nor will we owe
    Any, so cheap a death, as saying, Go;

Go; and if that word have not quite killed thee,
    Ease me with death, by bidding me go too.
Oh, if it have, let my word work on me,
    And a just office on a murderer do.
Except it be too late, to kill me so,
    Being double dead, going, and bidding, go.

ELIZABETH BISHOP

One Art

The art of losing isn't hard to master;
so many things seem filled with the intent
to be lost that their loss is no disaster.

Lose something every day. Accept the fluster
of lost door keys, the hour badly spent.
The art of losing isn't hard to master.

Then practice losing farther, losing faster:
places, and names, and where it was you meant
to travel. None of these will bring disaster.

I lost my mother's watch. And look! my last, or
next-to-last, of three loved houses went.
The art of losing isn't hard to master.

I lost two cities, lovely ones. And, vaster,
some realms I owned, two rivers, a continent.
I miss them, but it wasn't a disaster.

– Even losing you (the joking voice, a gesture
I love) I shan't have lied. It's evident
the art of losing's not too hard to master
though it may look like (*Write* it!) like disaster.

JAMES MERRILL
A Renewal

Having used every subterfuge
To shake you, lies, fatigue, or even that of passion,
Now I see no way but a clean break.
I add that I am willing to bear the guilt.

You nod assent. Autumn turns windy, huge,
A clear vase of dry leaves vibrating on and on.
We sit, watching. When I next speak
Love buries itself in me, up to the hilt.

ALICE MEYNELL

Renouncement

I must not think of thee; and, tired yet strong,
  I shun the thought that lurks in all delight –
The thought of thee – and in the blue Heaven's height,
And in the sweetest passage of a song.

O just beyond the fairest thoughts that throng
  This breast, the thought of thee waits, hidden yet bright;
  But it must never, never come in sight;
I must stop short of thee the whole day long.

But when sleep comes to close each difficult day,
  When night gives pause to the long watch I keep,
    And all my bonds I needs must loose apart,

Must doff my will as raiment laid away, –
  With the first dream that comes with the first sleep
    I run, I run, I am gathered to thy heart.

BRIAN PATTEN

I Have Changed the Numbers on My Watch

I have changed the numbers on my watch,
and now perhaps something else will change.
Now perhaps
at precisely 6 a.m.
you will not get up
and gathering your things together
go forever.
Perhaps now you will find it is
far too early to go,
or far too late,
and stay forever.

Needle on Zero

The unexpected power cut left the clocks
in every room regurgitating nought after nought –
you are leaving. The train approaches. Things start to shake.
The number of days and of nights
and the number of hours and of minutes, rattle over at speed
like the destinations on the departure board.
Look. The old world snaps like a wishbone.
As easy as that, with hardly a protest.
It was the words you spoke, so few, which left
the marital home as rubble and a fine dust to descend
like snow onto your shoes, wiped to a half moon.
And you step out from it – while every fin
of your watch's tiny universe begins to spin –
in new coat, high heels, your brilliant skin.

EDWARD THOMAS

'Go now'

Like the touch of rain she was
On a man's flesh and hair and eyes
When the joy of walking thus
Has taken him by surprise:

With the love of the storm he burns,
He sings, he laughs, well I know how,
But forgets when he returns
As I shall not forget her 'Go now'.

Those two words shut a door
Between me and the blessed rain
That was never shut before
And will not open again.

JUDITH RODRIGUEZ

In-flight Note

Kitten, writes the mousy boy in his neat
fawn casuals sitting beside me on the flight,
neatly, *I can't give up everything just like that.*
Everything, how much was it? and just like what?
Did she cool it or walk out? loosen her hand from his tight
white-knuckled hand, or not meet him, just as he thought

You mean far too much to me. I can't forget
the four months we've known each other. No, he won't
    eat,
finally he pays – pale, careful, distraught –
for a beer, turns over the pad on the page he wrote
and sleeps a bit. Or dreams of his Sydney cat.
The pad cost one dollar twenty. He wakes to write
It's naive to think we could be just good friends.
Pages and pages. And so the whole world ends.

SOPHIE HANNAH

The End of Love

The end of love should be a big event.
It should involve the hiring of a hall.
Why the hell not? It happens to us all.
Why should it pass without acknowledgement?

Suits should be dry-cleaned, invitations sent.
Whatever form it takes – a tiff, a brawl –
The end of love should be a big event.
It should involve the hiring of a hall.

Better than the unquestioning descent
Into the trap of silence, than the crawl
From visible to hidden, door to wall.

Get the announcements made, the money spent.
The end of love should be a big event.
It should involve the hiring of a hall.

Forsaken

MATTHEW SWEENEY

The Bridal Suite

For Nuala Ní Dhomnaill

On the third night in the bridal suite
without the bride, he panicked.
He couldn't handle another dream like that,
not wet, like he'd expected,
but not dry either – men digging holes
that they'd fill with water, donkeys
crossing valleys that suddenly flooded.
The alarm-call had a job to wake him,
to send him out from the huge bed,
past the corner kissing-sofa, up two steps
to the shower he hardly needed,
where he'd scrub himself clean as the baby
he'd hoped to start that night,
under the canopy like a wimple,
in that room of pinks and greens.
Naked and dripping, he'd rung Reception
to see if she'd rung, then he'd stood
looking out at the new marina,
as if he'd glimpse her on a yacht.
On the third night he could take no more –
he dressed, to the smell of her perfume,
and leaving her clothes there,
the wedding dress in a pile in the wardrobe,
he walked past the deaf night porter,
out to his car. He had no idea
where he was headed, only that she,
if she ever came back, could sample
the bridal suite on her own,
could toss in that canopied bed
and tell him about her dreams.

LADY AUGUSTA GREGORY,
TRANSLATED FROM THE IRISH
(ANONYMOUS)

Donal Og

It is late last night the dog was speaking of you;
the snipe was speaking of you in her deep marsh.
It is you are the lonely bird through the woods;
and that you may be without a mate until you find me.

You promised me, and you said a lie to me,
that you would be before me where the sheep are flocked;
I gave a whistle and three hundred cries to you,
and I found nothing there but a bleating lamb.

You promised me a thing that was hard for you,
a ship of gold under a silver mast;
twelve towns with a market in all of them,
and a fine white court by the side of the sea.

You promised me a thing that is not possible,
that you would give me gloves of the skin of a fish;
that you would give me shoes of the skin of a bird;
and a suit of the dearest silk in Ireland.

When I go by myself to the Well of Loneliness,
I sit down and I go through my trouble;
when I see the world and do not see my boy,
he that has an amber shade in his hair.

It was on that Sunday I gave my love to you;
the Sunday that is last before Easter Sunday.
And myself on my knees reading the Passion;
and my two eyes giving love to you for ever.

My mother said to me not to be talking with you today,
or tomorrow, or on the Sunday;
it was a bad time she took for telling me that;
it was shutting the door after the house was robbed.

My heart is as black as the blackness of the sloe,
or as the black coal that is on the smith's forge;
or as the sole of a shoe left in white halls;
it was you put that darkness over my life.

You have taken the east from me; you have taken the west from me;
you have taken what is before me and what is behind me;
you have taken the moon, you have taken the sun from me;
and my fear is great that you have taken God from me!

SIR WALTER RALEGH

As you came from the holy land
    Of Walsingham,
Met you not with my true love
    By the way as you came?

How shall I know your true love,
    That have met many one
As I went to the holy land,
    That have come, that have gone?

She is neither white nor brown
    But as the heavens fair,
There is none hath a form so divine
    In the earth or the air.

Such an one did I meet, good sir,
    Such an angelic face,
Who like a queen, like a nymph, did appear
    By her gait, by her grace.

She hath left me here all alone,
    All alone as unknown,
Who sometimes did me lead with herself,
    And me loved as her own.

What's the cause that she leaves you alone
    And a new way doth take,
Who loved you once as her own
    And her joy did you make?

I have loved her all my youth,
    But now old, as you see,
Love likes not the falling fruit
    From the withered tree.

Know that love is a careless child
        And forgets promise past,
He is blind, he is deaf when he list,
        And in faith never fast.

His desire is a dureless content
        And a trustless joy,
He is won with a world of despair
        And is lost with a toy.

Of women kind such indeed is the love,
        Or the word Love abused,
Under which many childish desires
        And conceits are excused.

But true love is a durable fire
        In the mind ever burning;
Never sick, never old, never dead,
        From itself never turning.

WILLIAM SOUTAR

The Tryst

O luely, luely cam she in
And luely she lay doun:
I kent her by her caller lips
And her breists sae sma' and roun'.

A' thru the nicht we spak nae word
Nor sinder'd bane frae bane:
A' thru the nicht I heard her hert
Gang soundin' wi' my ain.

It was about the waukrife hour
Whan cocks begin to craw
That she smool'd saftly thru the mirk
Afore the day wud daw.

Sae luely, luely, cam she in
Sae luely was she gaen
And wi' her a' my simmer days
Like they had never been.

FLEUR ADCOCK

Incident

When you were lying on the white sand,
a rock under your head, and smiling,
(circled by dead shells), I came to you
and you said, reaching to take my hand,
'Lie down.' So for a time we lay
warm on the sand, talking and smoking,
easy; while the grovelling sea behind
sucked at the rocks and measured the day.
Lightly I fell asleep then, and fell
into a cavernous dream of falling.
It was all the cave-myths, it was all
the myths of tunnel or tower or well –
Alice's rabbit-hole into the ground,
or the path of Orpheus: a spiral staircase
to hell, furnished with danger and doubt.
Stumbling, I suddenly woke; and found
water about me. My hair was wet,
and you were lying on the grey sand
waiting for the lapping tide to take me:
watching, and lighting a cigarette.

ANONYMOUS

The Water is Wide

The water is wide, I can't swim o'er
Nor do I have wings to fly
Give me a boat that can carry two
And both shall row, my love and I

A ship there is and she sails the sea
She's loaded deep as deep can be
But not so deep as the love I'm in
I know not if I sink or swim

I leaned my back against an oak
Thinking it was a trusty tree
But first it swayed and then it broke
So did my love prove false to me

Oh love is handsome and love is kind
Sweet as flower when first it is new
But love grows old and waxes cold
And fades away like the morning dew

Must I go bound while you go free
Must I love a man who doesn't love me
Must I be born with so little art
As to love a man who'll break my heart

A. E. HOUSMAN

He would not stay for me; and who can wonder?
   He would not stay for me to stand and gaze.
I shook his hand and tore my heart in sunder
   And went with half my life about my ways.

JACKIE KAY

Her

I had been told about her.
How she would always, always.
How she would never, never.
I'd watched and listened
but I still fell for her,
how she always, always.
How she never, never.

In the small brave night,
her lips, butterfly moments.
I tried to catch her and she laughed
a loud laugh that cracked me in two,
but then I had been told about her,
how she would always, always.
How she would never, never.

We two listened to the wind.
We two galloped a pace.
We two, up and away, away, away.
And now she's gone,
like she said she would go.
But then I had been told about her –
how she would always, always.

Regretfully

EDNA ST VINCENT MILLAY

When I too long have looked upon your face,
Wherein for me a brightness unobscured
Save by the mists of brightness has its place,
And terrible beauty not to be endured,
I turn away reluctant from your light,
And stand irresolute, a mind undone,
A silly, dazzled thing deprived of sight
From having looked too long upon the sun.
Then is my daily life a narrow room
In which a little while, uncertainly,
Surrounded by impenetrable gloom,
Among familiar things grown strange to me
Making my way, I pause, and feel, and hark,
Till I become accustomed to the dark.

MATTHEW SWEENEY

Cacti

After she left he bought another cactus
just like the one she'd bought him
in the airport in Marrakesh. He had to hunt
through London, and then, in Camden,
among hordes of hand-holding kids
who clog the market, he found it,
bought it, and brought it home to hers.
Next week he was back for another,
then another. He was coaxed into trying
different breeds, bright ones flashing red –
like the smile of the shop-girl
he hadn't noticed. He bought a rug, too,
sand-coloured, for the living-room,
and spent a weekend repainting
the walls beige, the ceiling pale blue.
He had the worn, black suite re-upholstered
in tan, and took to lying on the sofa
in a brown djellaba, with the cacti all around,
and Arab music on. If she should come back,
he thought, she might feel at home.

I want to talk to thee of many things
Or sit in silence when the robin sings
His little song, when comes the winter bleak
I want to sit beside thee, cheek to cheek.

I want to hear thy voice my name repeat,
To fill my heart with echoes ever sweet;
I want to hear thy love come calling me
I want to seek and find but thee, but thee.

I want to talk to thee of little things
So fond, so frail, so foolish that one clings
To keep them ours – who could but understand
A joy in speaking them, thus hand in hand

Beside the fire; our joys, our hopes, our fears,
Our secret laughter, or unchidden tears;
Each day old dreams come back with beating wings,
I want to speak of these forgotten things.

I want to feel thy arms around me pressed,
To hide my weeping eyes upon thy breast;
I want thy strength to hold and comfort me
For all the grief I had in losing thee.

JOHN CLARE

How Can I Forget

That farewell voice of love is never heard again,
Yet I remember it and think on it with pain:
I see the place she spoke when passing by,
The flowers were blooming as her form drew nigh,
That voice is gone, with every pleasing tone –
Loved but one moment and the next alone.
'Farewell' the winds repeated as she went
Walking in silence through the grassy bent;
The wild flowers – they ne'er looked so sweet before –
Bowed in farewells to her they'll see no more.
In this same spot the wild flowers bloom the same
In scent and hue and shape, ay, even name.
'Twas here she said farewell and no one yet
Has so sweet spoken – How can I forget?

LINTON KWESI JOHNSON

Hurricane Blues

langtime lovah
mi mine run pan yu all di while
an mi membah how fus time
di two a wi come een – it did seem
like two shallow likkle snakin stream
mawchin mapless hapless a galang
tru di ruggid lanscape a di awt sang

an a soh wi did a gwaan
sohtil dat fateful day
awftah di pashan a di hurricane
furdah dan imaginaeshan ar dream
wi fine wiself lay-dung pan di same bedrack
flowin now togedah as wan stream
ridin sublime tru love lavish terrain
lush an green an brite awftah di rain
shimmarin wid glittahrin eyes
glowin in di glare a di smilin sun

langtime lovah
mi feel blue fi true wen mi tink bout yu
blue like di sky lingahrin pramis af rain
in di leakin lite in di hush af a evenin twilite
wen mi membah how fus time
di two wi come een – it did seem
like a lang lang rivah dat is wide an deep

somtime wi woz silent like di langwidge a rackstone
somtime wi woodah sing wi rivah sang as wi a wine a galang
somtime wi jus cool an caam andah plenty shady tree
somtime sawfly lappin bamboo root as dem swing an sway
somtime cascadin carefree doun a steep gully bank
somtime turbulent in tempament wi flood wi bank
but weddah ebb ar flow tru rain tru drout
wi nevah stray far fram love rigid route

ole-time sweet-awt
up til now mi still cyaan andastan
ow wi get bag doun inna somuch silt an san
rackstone debri lag-jam
sohtil wi ad woz fi flow wi separet pawt
now traversin di tarrid terrain a love lanscape
runnin fram di polueshan af a cantrite awt
mi lang fi di marvelous miracle a hurricane
fi carry mi goh a meet in stream agen
lamentin mi saltid fate
sohmizin seh it too late

T. S. ELIOT

La Figlia Che Piange

O quam te memorem virgo . . .

Stand on the highest pavement of the stair –
Lean on a garden urn –
Weave, weave the sunlight in your hair –
Clasp your flowers to you with a pained surprise –
Fling them to the ground and turn
With a fugitive resentment in your eyes:
But weave, weave the sunlight in your hair.

So I would have had him leave,
So I would have had her stand and grieve,
So he would have left
As the soul leaves the body torn and bruised,
As the mind deserts the body it has used.
I should find
Some way incomparably light and deft,
Some way we both should understand,
Simple and faithless as a smile and shake of the hand.

She turned away, but with the autumn weather
Compelled my imagination many days,
Many days and many hours:
Her hair over her arms and her arms full of flowers.
And I wonder how they should have been together!
I should have lost a gesture and a pose.
Sometimes these cogitations still amaze
The troubled midnight and the noon's repose.

WILLIAM EMPSON

Villanelle

It is the pain, it is the pain, endures.
Your chemic beauty burned my muscles through.
Poise of my hands reminded me of yours.

What later purge from this deep toxin cures?
What kindness now could the old salve renew?
It is the pain, it is the pain, endures.

The infection slept (custom or change inures)
And when pain's secondary phase was due
Poise of my hands reminded me of yours.

How safe I felt, whom memory assures,
Rich that your grace safely by heart I knew.
It is the pain, it is the pain, endures.

My stare drank deep beauty that still allures.
My heart pumps yet the poison draught of you.
Poise of my hands reminded me of yours.

You are still kind whom the same shape immures.
Kind and beyond adieu. We miss our cue.
It is the pain, it is the pain, endures.
Poise of my hands reminded me of yours.

THOMAS HARDY

At Castle Boterel

As I drive to the junction of lane and highway,
   And the drizzle bedrenches the waggonette,
I look behind at the fading byway,
    And see on its slope, now glistening wet,
      Distinctly yet

Myself and a girlish form benighted
   In dry March weather. We climb the road
Beside a chaise. We had just alighted
    To ease the sturdy pony's load
      When he sighed and slowed.

What we did as we climbed, and what we talked of
   Matters not much, nor to what it led, –
Something that life will not be balked of
    Without rude reason till hope is dead,
      And feeling fled.

It filled but a minute. But was there ever
   A time of such quality, since or before,
In that hill's story? To one mind never,
    Though it has been climbed, foot-swift, foot-sore,
      By thousands more.

Primaeval rocks form the road's steep border,
   And much have they faced there, first and last,
Of the transitory in Earth's long order;
    But what they record in colour and cast
      Is – that we two passed.

And to me, though Time's unflinching rigour,
    In mindless rote, has ruled from sight
The substance now, one phantom figure
    Remains on the slope, as when that night
        Saw us alight.

I look and see it there, shrinking, shrinking,
    I look back at it amid the rain
For the very last time; for my sand is sinking,
    And I shall traverse old love's domain
        Never again.

VIKRAM SETH

Progress Report

My need has frayed with time; you said it would.
It has; I can walk again across the flood
Of gold silk poppies on the straw-gold hills
Under a deep Californian sky that expels
All truant clouds; watch squads of cattle graze
By the radio-telescope; blue-battered jays
Flash raucous squawking by my swivelling head
While squirrels sine-wave past over the dead
Oak-leaves, and not miss you – although I may
Admit that near the telescope yesterday
By a small bushcovered gully I blundered on
Five golden fox-cubs playing in the sun
And wished you had been there to see them play;
But that I only mention by the way.

GWEN HARWOOD

Anniversary

So the light falls, and so it fell
on branches leaved with flocking birds.
Light stole a city's weight to swell
the coloured life of stone. Your words
hung weightless in my ear: *Remember me.*

All words except those words were drowned
in the fresh babbling rush of spring.
In summer's dream-filled light one sound
echoed through all the whispering
galleries of green: *Remember me.*

Rods of light point home the flocking
starlings to wintry trees, and turn
stone into golden ochre, locking
the orbit of my pain. I learn
the weight of light and stone. Remember me.

DUNCAN FORBES

Recension Day

Unburn the boat, rebuild the bridge,
Reconsecrate the sacrilege,
Unspill the milk, decry the tears,
Turn back the clock, relive the years,
Replace the smoke inside the fire,
Unite fulfilment with desire,
Undo the done, gainsay the said,
Revitalise the buried dead,
Revoke the penalty and clause,
Reconstitute unwritten laws,
Repair the heart, untie the tongue,
Change faithless old to hopeful young,
Inure the body to disease
And help me to forget you please.

Fatally

SIR HENRY WOTTON

Upon the Death of Sir Albert Morton's Wife

He first deceased: She for a little tried
To live without Him: liked it not, and died.

OSCAR WILDE

from The Ballad of Reading Gaol

Yet each man kills the thing he loves,
  By each let this be heard,
Some do it with a bitter look,
  Some with a flattering word,
The coward does it with a kiss,
  The brave man with a sword!

Some kill their love when they are young,
  And some when they are old;
Some strangle with the hands of Lust,
  Some with the hands of Gold:
The kindest use a knife, because
  The dead so soon grow cold.

Some love too little, some too long,
  Some sell, and others buy;
Some do the deed with many tears,
  And some without a sigh:
For each man kills the thing he loves.
  Yet each man does not die.

WILLIAM SHAKESPEARE

from *Othello*, V, ii

Desdemona in her bed. Enter OTHELLO *with a light.*
OTHELLO:
    It is the cause, it is the cause, my soul:
    Let me not name it to you, you chaste stars!
    It is the cause. Yet I'll not shed her blood,
    Nor scar that whiter skin of hers than snow,
    And smooth as monumental alabaster:
    Yet she must die, else she'll betray more men.
    Put out the light, and then put out the light:
    If I quench thee, thou flaming minister,
    I can again thy former light restore,
    Should I repent me; but once put out thy light,
    Thou cunning'st pattern of excelling nature,
    I know not where is that Promethean heat
    That can thy light relume. When I have plucked thy rose,
    I cannot give it vital growth again,
    It needs must wither. I'll smell it on the tree.
       He kisses her.
    O balmy breath, that dost almost persuade
    Justice to break her sword! One more, one more.
    Be thus when thou art dead and I will kill thee,
    And love thee after. One more, and this the last.
    So sweet was ne'er so fatal. I must weep.
    But they are cruel tears: this sorrow's heavenly –
    It strikes where it doth love.

ROBERT BROWNING

Porphyria's Lover

The rain set early in tonight,
   The sullen wind was soon awake,
It tore the elm-tops down for spite,
   And did its worst to vex the lake:
   I listened with heart fit to break.
When glided in Porphyria; straight
   She shut the cold out and the storm,
And kneeled and made the cheerless grate
   Blaze up, and all the cottage warm;
   Which done, she rose, and from her form
Withdrew the dripping cloak and shawl,
   And laid her soiled gloves by, untied
Her hat and let the damp hair fall,
   And, last, she sat down by my side
   And called me. When no voice replied,
She put my arm about her waist,
   And made her smooth white shoulder bare,
And all her yellow hair displaced,
   And, stooping, made my cheek lie there,
   And spread, o'er all, her yellow hair,
Murmuring how she loved me – she
   Too weak, for all her heart's endeavour,
To set its struggling passion free
   From pride, and vainer ties dissever,
   And give herself to me for ever.
But passion sometimes would prevail,
   Nor could tonight's gay feast restrain
A sudden thought of one so pale
   For love of her, and all in vain:
   So, she was come through wind and rain.

Be sure I looked up at her eyes
 Happy and proud; at last I knew
Porphyria worshipped me; surprise
 Made my heart swell, and still it grew
 While I debated what to do.
That moment she was mine, mine, fair,
 Perfectly pure and good: I found
A thing to do, and all her hair
 In one long yellow string I wound
 Three times her little throat around,
And strangled her. No pain felt she;
 I am quite sure she felt no pain.
As a shut bud that holds a bee,
 I warily oped her lids: again
 Laughed the blue eyes without a stain.
And I untightened next the tress
 About her neck; her cheek once more
Blushed bright beneath my burning kiss:
 I propped her head up as before,
 Only, this time my shoulder bore
Her head, which droops upon it still:
 The smiling rosy little head,
So glad it has its utmost will,
 That all it scorned at once is fled,
 And I, its love, am gained instead!
Porphyria's love: she guessed not how
 Her darling one wish would be heard.
And thus we sit together now,
 And all night long we have not stirred,
 And yet God has not said a word!

ALFRED NOYES

The Highwayman

The wind was a torrent of darkness among the gusty trees,
The moon was a ghostly galleon tossed upon cloudy seas,
The road was a ribbon of moonlight over the purple moor,
And the highwayman came riding –
      Riding – riding –
The highwayman came riding, up to the old inn-door.

He'd a French cocked-hat on his forehead, a bunch of lace at his chin,
A coat of claret velvet, and breeches of brown doe-skin;
They fitted with never a wrinkle: his boots were up to the thigh!
And he rode with a jewelled twinkle,
      His pistol butts a-twinkle,
His rapier hilt a-twinkle, under the jewelled sky.

Over the cobbles he clattered and clashed in the dark inn-yard,
And he tapped with his whip on the shutters, but all was locked and
        barred;
He whistled a tune to the window, and who should be waiting there
But the landlord's black-eyed daughter,
      Bess, the landlord's daughter,
Plaiting a dark red love-knot into her long black hair.

And dark in the old inn-yard a stable-wicket creaked
Where Tim the ostler listened; his face was white and peaked;
His eyes were hollows of madness, his hair like mouldy hay,
But he loved the landlord's daughter,
      The landlord's red-lipped daughter;
Dumb as a dog he listened, and he heard the robber say –

'One kiss, my bonny sweetheart, I'm after a prize to-night,
But I shall be back with the yellow gold before the morning light;

Yet, if they press me sharply, and harry me through the day,
Then look for me by moonlight,
     Watch for me by moonlight,
I'll come to thee by moonlight, though hell should bar the way.'

He rose upright in the stirrups; he scarce could reach her hand,
But she loosened her hair i' the casement! His face burnt like a brand
As the black cascade of perfume came tumbling over his breast;
And he kissed its waves in the moonlight,
     (Oh, sweet black waves in the moonlight!)
Then he tugged at his rein in the moonlight, and galloped away to the
        west.

II

He did not come in the dawning; he did not come at noon;
And out o' the tawny sunset, before the rise o' the moon,
When the road was a gipsy's ribbon, looping the purple moor,
A red-coat troop came marching –
     Marching – marching –
King George's men came marching, up to the old inn-door.

They said no word to the landlord, they drank his ale instead,
But they gagged his daughter and bound her to the foot of her
        narrow bed;
Two of them knelt at her casement, with muskets at their side!
There was death at every window;
     And hell at one dark window;
For Bess could see, through her casement, the road that *he* would
        ride.

They had tied her up to attention, with many a sniggering jest;
They had bound a musket beside her, with the barrel beneath her
        breast!
'Now keep good watch!' and they kissed her.
     She heard the dead man say –
Look for me by moonlight;
     Watch for me by moonlight;
I'll come to thee by moonlight, though hell should bar the way!

She twisted her hands behind her; but all the knots held good!
She writhed her hands till her fingers were wet with sweat or
        blood!
They stretched and strained in the darkness, and the hours
        crawled by like years,
Till, now, on the stroke of midnight,
      Cold, on the stroke of midnight,
The tip of one finger touched it! The trigger at least was hers!

The tip of one finger touched it; she strove no more for the rest!
Up, she stood to attention, with the barrel beneath her breast,
She would not risk their hearing; she would not strive again;
For the road lay bare in the moonlight;
      Blank and bare in the moonlight;
And the blood of her veins in the moonlight throbbed to her
        love's refrain.

Tlot-tlot; tlot-tlot! Had they heard it? The horse-hoofs ringing
        clear;
Tlot-tlot, tlot-tlot, in the distance? Where they deaf that they did
        not hear?
Down the ribbon of moonlight, over the brow of the hill,
The highwayman came riding,
      Riding, riding!
The red-coats looked to their priming! She stood up, straight and
        still!

Tlot-tlot, in the frosty silence! *tlot-tlot*, in the echoing night!
Nearer he came and nearer! Her face was like a light!
Her eyes grew wide for a moment; she drew one last deep breath,
Then her finger moved in the moonlight,
      Her musket shattered the moonlight,
Shattered her breast in the moonlight and warned him – with her
        death.

He turned; he spurred to the westward; he did not know who
        stood
Bowed, with her head o'er the musket, drenched with her own
        red blood!

Not till the dawn he heard it, and slowly blanched to hear
How Bess, the landlord's daughter,
  The landlord's black-eyed daughter,
Had watched for her love in the moonlight, and died in the
   darkness there.

Back, he spurred like a madman, shrieking a curse to the sky,
With the white road smoking behind him and his rapier
   brandished high!
Blood-red were his spurs i' the golden noon; wine-red was his
   velvet coat;
When they shot him down on the highway,
  Down like a dog on the highway,
And he lay in his blood on the highway, with the bunch of lace at
   his throat.

And still of a winter's night, they say, when the wind is in the
   trees,
When the moon is a ghostly galleon tossed upon cloudy seas,
When the road is a ribbon of moonlight over the purple moor,
A highwayman comes riding –
  Riding – riding –
A highwayman comes riding, up to the old inn-door.

Over the cobbles he clatters and clangs in the dark inn-yard
And he taps with his whip on the shutters, but all is locked and
   barred;
He whistles a tune to the window, and who should be waiting
   there
But the landlord's black-eyed daughter,
  Bess, the landlord's daughter,
Plaiting a dark red love-knot into her long black hair.

OLIVER GOLDSMITH

from *The Vicar of Wakefield*

When lovely woman stoops to folly,
    And finds too late that men betray,
What charm can sooth her melancholy,
    What art can wash her guilt away?

The only art her guilt to cover,
    To hide her shame from every eye,
To give repentance to her lover,
    And wring his bosom, is – to die.

ALFRED, LORD TENNYSON

The Lady of Shalott

PART I

On either side the river lie
Long fields of barley and of rye,
That clothe the wold and meet the sky;
And thro' the field the road runs by
    To many-tower'd Camelot;
And up and down the people go,
Gazing where the lilies blow
Round an island there below,
    The island of Shalott.

Willows whiten, aspens quiver,
Little breezes dusk and shiver
Thro' the wave that runs for ever
By the island in the river
    Flowing down to Camelot.
Four gray walls, and four gray towers,
Overlook a space of flowers,
And the silent isle imbowers
    The Lady of Shalott.

By the margin, willow-veil'd,
Slide the heavy barges trail'd
By slow horses; and unhail'd
The shallop flitteth silken-sail'd
    Skimming down to Camelot;
But who hath seen her wave her hand?
Or at the casement seen her stand?
Or is she known in all the land,
    The Lady of Shalott?

Only reapers, reaping early
In among the bearded barley,
Hear a song that echoes cheerly
From the river winding clearly,
        Down to tower'd Camelot:
And by the moon the reaper weary,
Piling sheaves in uplands airy,
Listening, whispers ''Tis the fairy
        Lady of Shalott.'

PART II

There she weaves by night and day
A magic web with colours gay.
She has heard a whisper say,
A curse is on her if she stay
        To look down to Camelot.
She knows not what the curse may be,
And so she weaveth steadily,
And little other care hath she,
        The Lady of Shalott.

And moving thro' a mirror clear
That hangs before her all the year,
Shadows of the world appear.
There she sees the highway near
        Winding down to Camelot:
There the river eddy whirls,
And there the surly village-churls,
And the red cloaks of market girls,
        Pass onward from Shalott.

Sometimes a troop of damsels glad,
An abbot on an ambling pad,
Sometimes a curly shepherd-lad
Or long-hair'd page in crimson clad,
        Goes by to tower'd Camelot;

And sometimes thro' the mirror blue
The knights come riding two and two:
She hath no loyal knight and true,
  The Lady of Shalott.

But in her web she still delights
To weave the mirror's magic sights,
For often thro' the silent nights
A funeral, with plumes and lights
  And music, went to Camelot:
Or when the moon was overhead,
Came two young lovers lately wed;
'I am half sick of shadows,' said
  The Lady of Shalott.

PART III

A bow-shot from her bower-eaves,
He rode between the barley-sheaves,
The sun came dazzling thro' the leaves,
And flamed upon the brazen greaves
  Of bold Sir Lancelot.
A red-cross knight for ever kneel'd
To a lady in his shield,
That sparkled on the yellow field,
  Beside remote Shalott.

The gemmy bridle glitter'd free,
Like to some branch of stars we see
Hung in the golden Galaxy.
The bridle bells rang merrily
  As he rode down to Camelot:
And from his blazon'd baldric slung
A mighty silver bugle hung,
And as he rode his armour rung,
  Beside remote Shalott.

All in the blue unclouded weather
Thick-jewell'd shone the saddle-leather,
The helmet and the helmet-feather
Burn'd like one burning flame together,
     As he rode down to Camelot.
As often thro' the purple night,
Below the starry clusters bright,
Some bearded meteor, trailing light,
     Moves over still Shalott.

His broad clear brow in sunlight glow'd;
On burnish'd hooves his war-horse trode;
From underneath his helmet flow'd
His coal-black curls as on he rode,
     As he rode down to Camelot.
From the bank and from the river
He flash'd into the crystal mirror,
'Tirra lirra,' by the river
     Sang Sir Lancelot.

She left the web, she left the loom,
She made three paces thro' the room,
She saw the water-lily bloom,
She saw the helmet and the plume,
     She look'd down to Camelot.
Out flew the web and floated wide;
The mirror crack'd from side to side;
'The curse is come upon me,' cried
     The Lady of Shalott.

PART IV

In the stormy east-wind straining,
The pale yellow woods were waning,
The broad stream in his banks complaining,
Heavily the low sky raining
     Over tower'd Camelot;

Down she came and found a boat
Beneath a willow left afloat,
And round about the prow she wrote
The Lady of Shalott.

And down the river's dim expanse
Like some bold seër in a trance,
Seeing all his own mischance –
With a glassy countenance
      Did she look to Camelot.
And at the closing of the day
She loosed the chain, and down she lay;
The broad stream bore her far away,
      The Lady of Shalott.

Lying, robed in snowy white
That loosely flew to left and right –
The leaves upon her falling light –
Thro' the noises of the night
      She floated down to Camelot:
And as the boat-head wound along
The willowy hills and fields among,
They heard her singing her last song,
      The Lady of Shalott.

Heard a carol, mournful, holy,
Chanted loudly, chanted lowly,
Till her blood was frozen slowly,
And her eyes were darken'd wholly,
      Turn'd to tower'd Camelot.
For ere she reach'd upon the tide
The first house by the water-side,
Singing in her song she died,
      The Lady of Shalott.

Under tower and balcony,
By garden-wall and gallery,
A gleaming shape she floated by,
Dead-pale between the houses high,
     Silent into Camelot.
Out upon the wharfs they came,
Knight and burgher, lord and dame,
And round the prow they read her name,
     The Lady of Shalott.

Who is this? and what is here?
And in the lighted palace near
Died the sound of royal cheer;
And they cross'd themselves for fear,
     All the knights at Camelot:
But Lancelot mused a little space;
He said, 'She has a lovely face;
God in his mercy lend her grace,
     The Lady of Shalott.'

VICKI FEAVER

Lily pond

Thinking of new ways to kill you
and bring you back from the dead,
I try drowning you in the lily pond –

holding your head down
until every bubble of breath
is squeezed from your lungs

and the flat leaves and spiky flowers
float over you like a wreath.
I sit on the stones until I'm numb,

until, among reflections of sky,
water-buttercups, spears of iris,
your face rises to the surface –

a face that was always puffy
and pale, so curiously unchanged.
A wind rocks the waxy flowers, curls

the edges of the leaves. Blue dragonflies
appear and vanish like ghosts.
I part the mats of yellow weed

and drag you to the bank, covering
your green algae-stained corpse
with a white sheet. Then, I lift the edge

and climb underneath –
thumping your chest,
breathing into your mouth.

ANNE FINCH, COUNTESS
OF WINCHILSEA

La Passion Vaincue

On the banks of the Severn, a desperate maid
(Whom some shepherd, neglecting his vows, had betrayed),
Stood resolving to banish all sense of the pain,
And pursue, thro' her death, a revenge on the swain.
'Since the gods and my passion at once he defies;
Since his vanity lives, while my character dies;
No more', did she say, 'will I trifle with fate,
But commit to the waves both my love and my hate.'
And now to comply with that furious desire,
Just ready to plunge, and alone to expire,
Some reflections on death and its terrors untried,
Some scorn for the shepherd, some flashings of pride
At length pulled her back, and she cried, 'Why this strife,
Since the swains are so many, and I've but *one* life?'

Indifferently

WENDY COPE

Loss

The day he moved out was terrible –
That evening she went through hell.
His absence wasn't a problem
But the corkscrew had gone as well.

SIR THOMAS WYATT

Farewell Love, and all thy laws for ever!
Thy baited hooks shall tangle me no more:
Senec and Plato call me from thy lore,
To perfect wealth my wit for to endeavour.
In blind error when I did persever,
Thy sharp repulse, that pricketh aye so sore,
Hath taught me to set in trifles no store,
And 'scape forth, since liberty is liever.
Therefore farewell! Go trouble younger hearts,
And in me claim no more authority;
With idle youth go use thy property,
And thereon spend thy many brittle darts:
For hitherto though I have lost all my time,
Me lusteth no longer rotten boughs to climb.

EDITH NESBIT

Villeggiature

My window, framed in pear-tree bloom,
    White-curtained shone, and softly lighted:
So, by the pear-tree, to my room
    Your ghost last night climbed uninvited.

Your solid self, long leagues away,
    Deep in dull books, had hardly missed me;
And yet you found this Romeo's way,
    And through the blossom climbed and kissed me.

I watched the still and dewy lawn,
    The pear-tree boughs hung white above you;
I listened to you till the dawn,
    And half forgot I did not love you.

Oh, dear! what pretty things you said,
    What pearls of song you threaded for me!
I did not – till your ghost had fled –
    Remember how you always bore me!

HENRY KING

The Double Rock

Since thou hast view'd some Gorgon, and art grown
    A solid stone:
To bring again to softness thy hard heart
    Is past my art.
Ice may relent to water in a thaw;
But stone made flesh Love's Chemistry ne're saw.

Therefore by thinking on thy hardness, I
    Will petrify;
And so within our double Quarries' Womb,
    Dig our Love's Tomb.
Thus strangely will our difference agree;
And, with our selves, amaze the world, to see
How both Revenge and Sympathy consent
To make two Rocks each others Monument.

A. E. HOUSMAN

from *A Shropshire Lad*

XVIII

Oh, when I was in love with you,
    Then I was clean and brave,
And miles around the wonder grew
    How well did I behave.

And now the fancy passes by,
    And nothing will remain,
And miles around they'll say that I
    Am quite myself again.

GEOFFREY CHAUCER

from *Merciles Beaute*

III [ESCAPE]

Sin I fro Love escaped am so fat,
I never thenk to ben in his prison lene;
Sin I am free, I counte him not a bene.

He may answere, and seye this or that;
I do no fors, I speke right as I mene.
 Sin I fro Love escaped am so fat,
 I never thenk to ben in his prison lene.

Love hath my name ystrike out of his sclat,
And he is strike out of my bokes clene
For ever-mo; ther is non other mene.
 Sin I fro Love escaped am so fat,
 I never thenk to ben in his prison lene;
 Sin I am free, I counte him not a bene.

STEPHEN DUNN

Each from Different Heights

That time I thought I was in love
and calmly said so
was not much different from the time
I was truly in love
and slept poorly and spoke out loud
to the wall
and discovered the hidden genius
of my hands.
And the times I felt less in love,
less than someone,
were, to be honest, not so different
either.
Each was ridiculous in its own way
and each was tender, yes,
sometimes even the false is tender.
I am astounded
by the various kisses we're capable of.
Each from different heights
diminished, which is simply the law.
And the big bruise
from the longer fall looked perfectly white
in a few years.
That astounded me most of all.

CHARLOTTE MEW

I So Liked Spring

I so liked Spring last year
Because you were here; –
The thrushes too –
Because it was these you so liked to hear –
I so liked you –

This year's a different thing, –
I'll not think of you –
But I'll like Spring because it is simply Spring
As the thrushes do.

DEREK WALCOTT

Love after Love

The time will come
when, with elation,
you will greet yourself arriving
at your own door, in your own mirror,
and each will smile at the other's welcome,

and say, sit here. Eat.
You will love again the stranger who was your self.
Give wine. Give bread. Give back your heart
to itself, to the stranger who has loved you

all your life, whom you ignored
for another, who knows you by heart.
Take down the love letters from the bookshelf,

the photographs, the desperate notes,
peel your own image from the mirror.
Sit. Feast on your life.

After death

Hands

We first recognised each other as if we were siblings,
and when we held hands your touch
made me stupidly happy.

Hold my hand, you said in the hospital.

You had big hands, strong hands, gentle
as those of a Mediterranean father
caressing the head of a child.

Hold my hand, you said. *I feel
I won't die while you are here.*

You took my hand on our first aeroplane
and in opera houses, or watching
a video you wanted me to share.

Hold my hand, you said. *I'll fall asleep
and won't even know you're not there.*

R. S. THOMAS

A Marriage

We met
     under a shower
of bird-notes.
       Fifty years passed,
love's moment
     in a world in
servitude to time.
       She was young;
I kissed with my eyes
     closed and opened
them on her wrinkles.
       'Come,' said death,
choosing her as his
     partner for
the last dance. And she,
     who in life
had done everything
     with a bird's grace,
opened her bill now
     for the shedding
of one sigh no
       heavier than a feather.

Music, when soft voices die,
Vibrates in the memory –
Odours, when sweet violets sicken,
Live within the sense they quicken.

Rose leaves, when the rose is dead,
Are heaped for the belovèd's bed;
And so thy thoughts, when thou art gone,
Love itself shall slumber on.

WILLIAM MORRIS

Summer Dawn

Pray but one prayer for me 'twixt thy closed lips,
  Think but one thought of me up in the stars.
The summer night waneth, the morning light slips,
  Faint and grey 'twixt the leaves of the aspen, betwixt the
    cloud-bars,
That are patiently waiting there for the dawn:
  Patient and colourless, though Heaven's gold
Waits to float through them along with the sun.
Far out in the meadows, above the young corn,
  The heavy elms wait, and restless and cold
The uneasy wind rises; the roses are dun;
Through the long twilight they pray for the dawn,
Round the lone house in the midst of the corn.
  Speak but one word to me over the corn,
  Over the tender, bow'd locks of the corn.

THOMAS HARDY

The Voice

Woman much missed, how you call to me, call to me,
Saying that now you are not as you were
When you had changed from the one who was all to me,
But as at first, when our day was fair.

Can it be you that I hear? Let me view you, then,
Standing as when I drew near to the town
Where you would wait for me: yes, as I knew you then,
Even to the original air-blue gown!

Or is it only the breeze, in its listlessness
Travelling across the wet mead to me here,
You being ever dissolved to wan wistlessness,
Heard no more again far or near?

    Thus I; faltering forward,
    Leaves around me falling,
Wind oozing thin through the thorn from norward,
    And the woman calling.

DOUGLAS DUNN

Reincarnations

The kitten that befriends me at its gate
Purrs, rubs against me, until I say goodbye,
Stroking its coat, and asking 'Why? Why? Why?'
For now I know the shame of being late
Too late. She waits for me at home
Tonight, in the house-shadows. And I must mourn
Until Equator crawls to Capricorn
Or murder in the sun melts down
The Arctic and Antarctica. When bees collide
Against my study's windowpane, I let them in.
She nurtures dignity and pride;
She waters in my eye. She rustles in my study's palm;
She is the flower on the geranium.
Our little wooden train runs by itself
Along the windowsill, each puff-puff-puff
A breath of secret, sacred stuff.
I feel her goodness breathe, my Lady Christ.
Her treasured stories mourn her on their shelf,
In spirit-air, that watchful poltergeist.

JOHN MILTON

Methought I saw my late espousèd saint
  Brought to me like Alcestis from the grave,
  Whom Jove's great son to her glad husband gave,
  Rescued from death by force though pale and faint.
Mine as whom washed from spot of childbed taint,
  Purification in the old Law did save,
  And such, as yet once more I trust to have
  Full sight of her in Heaven without restraint,
Came vested all in white, pure as her mind:
  Her face was veiled, yet to my fancied sight,
  Love, sweetness, goodness, in her person shined
So clear, as in no face with more delight.
  But O as to embrace me she inclined
  I waked, she fled, and day brought back my night.

WILLIAM SHAKESPEARE

from *Antony and Cleopatra*, V, ii

CLEOPATRA:
 I dreamt there was an emperor Antony.
 O, such another sleep, that I might see
 But such another man!
DOLABELLA: If it might please ye –
CLEOPATRA:
 His face was as the heavens, and therein stuck
 A sun and moon, which kept their course and lighted
 The little O o'th'earth.
DOLABELLA: Most sovereign creature –
CLEOPATRA:
 His legs bestrid the ocean; his reared arm
 Crested the world; his voice was propertied
 As all the tunèd spheres, and that to friends;
 But when he meant to quail and shake the orb,
 He was as rattling thunder. For his bounty,
 There was no winter in't; an Antony it was
 That grew the more by reaping. His delights
 Were dolphin-like; they showed his back above
 The element they lived in. In his livery
 Walked crowns and crownets; realms and islands were
 As plates dropped from his pocket.
DOLABELLA: Cleopatra –
CLEOPATRA:
 Think you there was or might be such a man
 As this I dreamt of?
DOLABELLA: Gentle madam, no.
CLEOPATRA:
 You lie, up to the hearing of the gods.
 But if there be nor ever were one such,
 It's past the size of dreaming. Nature wants stuff
 To vie strange forms with fancy, yet t'imagine
 An Antony were nature's piece 'gainst fancy,
 Condemning shadows quite.

WILLIAM BARNES

The Wife A-Lost

Since I noo mwore do zee your feäce,
    Up steäirs or down below,
I'll zit me in the lwonesome pleäce,
    Where flat-bough'd beech do grow;
Below the beeches' bough, my love,
    Where you did never come,
An' I don't look to meet ye now,
    As I do look at hwome.

Since you noo mwore be at my zide,
    In walks in zummer het,
I'll goo alwone where mist do ride,
    Drough trees a-drippen wet;
Below the raïn-wet bough, my love,
    Where you did never come,
An' I don't grieve to miss ye now,
    As I do grieve at hwome.

Since now bezide my dinner-bwoard
    Your vaïce do never sound,
I'll eat the bit I can avvword,
    A-yield upon the ground;
Below the darksome bough, my love,
    Where you did never dine,
An' I don't grieve to miss ye now,
    As I at hwome do pine.

Since I do miss your vaïce an' feäce
    In praÿer at eventide,
I'll praÿ wi' woone sad vaïce vor greäce
    To goo where you do bide;
Above the tree an' bough, my love,
    Where you be gone avore,
An' be a-waïten vor me now,
    To come vor evermwore.

EDGAR ALLAN POE

Annabel Lee

It was many and many a year ago,
　　In a kingdom by the sea
That a maiden there lived whom you may know
　　By the name of Annabel Lee:
And this maiden she lived with no other thought
　　Than to love and be loved by me.

I was a child and *she* was a child,
　　In this kingdom by the sea,
But we loved with a love that was more than love –
　　I and my Annabel Lee –
With a love that the wingèd seraphs of heaven
　　Coveted her and me.

And this was the reason that, long ago,
　　In this kingdom by the sea,
A wind blew out of a cloud, chilling
　　My beautiful Annabel Lee;
So that her highborn kinsmen came
　　And bore her away from me,
To shut her up in a sepulchre
　　In this kingdom by the sea.

The angels, not half so happy in heaven,
　　Went envying her and me –
Yes! – that was the reason (as all men know,
　　In this kingdom by the sea)
That the wind came out of the cloud by night,
　　Chilling and killing my Annabel Lee.

But our love it was stronger by far than the love
    Of those who were older than we –
    Of many far wiser than we –
And neither the angels in heaven above,
    Nor the demons down under the sea,
Can ever dissever my soul from the soul
    Of the beautiful Annabel Lee:

For the moon never beams, without bringing me dreams
    Of the beautiful Annabel Lee;
And the stars never rise, but I feel the bright eyes
    Of the beautiful Annabel Lee;
And so, all the night-tide, I lie down by the side
Of my darling – my darling – my life and my bride,
    In her sepulchre there by the sea –
    In her tomb by the sounding sea.

HENRY KING

from *The Exequy*

So close the ground, and 'bout her shade
Black curtains draw; my bride is laid.
  Sleep on, my love, in thy cold bed
Never to be disquieted!
My last goodnight! Thou wilt not wake
Till I thy fate shall overtake:
Till age, or grief, or sickness must
Marry my body to that dust
It so much loves; and fill the room
My heart keeps empty in thy tomb.
Stay for me there; I will not fail
To meet thee in that hollow vale.
And think not much of my delay;
I am already on the way,
And follow thee with all the speed
Desire can make, or sorrows breed.
Each minute is a short degree,
And ev'ry hour a step towards thee.
At night when I betake to rest,
Next morn I rise nearer my west
Of life, almost by eight hours' sail,
Than when sleep breathed his drowsy gale.
  Thus from the sun my bottom steers,
And my day's compass downward bears:
Nor labour I to stem the tide
Through which to thee I swiftly glide.
  'Tis true, with shame and grief I yield,
Thou like the van first took'st the field,
And gotten hast the victory
In thus adventuring to die
Before me, whose more years might crave
A just precedence in the grave.

But hark! My pulse like a soft drum
Beats my approach, tells thee I come;
And slow howe'er my marches be,
I shall at last sit down by thee.

    The thought of this bids me go on,
And wait my dissolution
With hope and comfort. Dear (forgive
The crime) I am content to live
Divided, with but half a heart,
Till we shall meet and never part.

Eternally

MARGARET ATWOOD

Sunset II

Sunset, now that we're finally in it
is not what we thought.

Did you expect this violet black
soft edge to outer space, fragile as blown ash
and shuddering like oil, or the reddish
orange that flows into
your lungs and through your fingers?
The waves smooth mouthpink light
over your eyes, fold after fold.
This is the sun you breathe in,
pale blue. Did you
expect it to be this warm?

One more goodbye,
sentimental as they all are.
The far west recedes from us
like a mauve postcard of itself
and dissolves into the sea.

Now there's a moon,
an irony. We walk
north towards no home,
joined at the hand.

I'll love you forever,
I can't stop time.

This is you on my skin somewhere
in the form of sand.

EDMUND SPENSER

from *Amoretti*

LXXV

One day I wrote her name upon the strand,
    but came the waves and washed it away;
    again I wrote it with a second hand,
    but came the tide, and made my pains his prey.
Vain man, said she, that dost in vain assay
    a mortal thing so to immortalize
    for I my self shall like to this decay,
    and eek my name be wiped out likewise.
Not so, (quoth I) let baser things devise
    to die in dust, but you shall live by fame:
    my verse your virtues rare shall eternise,
    and in the heavens write your glorious name:
Where, whenas death shall all the world subdue,
    Our love shall live, and later life renew.

ELIZABETH BARRETT BROWNING

from *Sonnets from the Portuguese*

XIV

If thou must love me, let it be for nought
Except for love's sake only. Do not say
'I love her for her smile ... her look ... her way
Of speaking gently, ... for a trick of thought
That falls in well with mine, and certes brought
A sense of pleasant ease on such a day' –
For these things in themselves, Belovèd, may
Be changed, or change for thee, – and love, so wrought
May be unwrought so. Neither love me for
Thine own dear pity's wiping my cheeks dry, –
A creature might forget to weep, who bore
Thy comfort long, and lose thy love thereby!
But love me for love's sake, that evermore
Thou may'st love on, through love's eternity.

ALFRED, LORD TENNYSON

If I were loved, as I desire to be,
What is there in this great sphere of earth,
And range of evil between death and birth,
That I should fear, – if I were loved by thee?
All the inner, all the outer world of pain
Clear love would pierce and cleave, if thou wert mine,
As I have heard that, somewhere in the main,
Fresh-water springs come up through bitter brine.
'Twere joy, not fear, clasped hand in hand with thee,
To wait for death – mute – careless of all ills,
Apart upon a mountain, though the surge
Of some new deluge from a thousand hills
Flung leagues of roaring foam into the gorge
Below us, as far on as eye could see.

EMILY DICKINSON

I have no Life but this –
To lead it here –
Nor any Death – but lest
Dispelled from there –

Nor tie to Earths to come –
Nor Action new –
Except through this extent –
The Realm of you –

LEONARD COHEN

Dance Me to the End of Love

Dance me to your beauty
with a burning violin
Dance me through the panic
till I'm gathered safely in
Lift me like an olive branch
and be my homeward dove
Dance me to the end of love

Let me see your beauty
when the witnesses are gone
Let me feel you moving
like they do in Babylon
Show me slowly what I only
know the limits of
Dance me to the end of love

Dance me to the wedding now
dance me on and on
Dance me very tenderly and
dance me very long
We're both of us beneath our love
we're both of us above
Dance me to the end of love

Dance me to the children
who are asking to be born
Dance me through the curtains
that our kisses have outworn
Raise a tent of shelter now
though every thread is torn
Dance me to the end of love

Dance me to your beauty
with a burning violin
Dance me through the panic
till I'm gathered safely in
Touch me with your naked hand
touch me with your glove
Dance me to the end of love

Acknowledgements

I owe my thanks and the promised chocolate heart to the following people for sharing their favourite love poems with me and also, in many cases, for their kind support and practical help: Claire Allfree, Ellah Allfrey, Ronald Asprey, Jo Baker, Diane Bourke, Tricia Bovis, Stephen Brown, Chloe Campbell, Isobel Dixon, Edward Docx, Amber Dowell, Sasha Dugdale, Ben Faccini, William Fiennes, Jamie Glazebrook, Anouchka Grose, Catherine Hall, Judith Heale, Denis Hirson, Robbie Hudson, Kevin Jackson, Clive James, Reina James, Philip Gwyn Jones, Kapka Kassabova, Paul Kingsnorth, Ian Knapp, Sarah Knight, Deborah Landau, Hilary Laurie, Molly Mackey, Anne Marsella, Hannah Marshall, Olivia McCannon, Richard Meier, Juliette Mitchell, Victoria Moore, Parashkev Nachev, Adriana Natcheva, Raj Patel, Lindsay Paterson, Alex Peake-Tomkinson, Michal Shavit, Anna Stein, Andrea Stuart, Hugh Warwick, Louis Watt, Joanna Weinberg, and Thomas Wright.

And at Penguin, thanks to Adam Freudenheim, Rachel Love, Elisabeth Merriman, Coralie Bickford-Smith, and Kristina Blagojevitch.

I dedicate this volume to my parents John and Susan Barber, and to my sister Florence, gratefully and always.

GALWAY KINNELL; 'Kissing the Toad' from *New Selected Poems* (Houghton Mifflin, 2000). Copyright © 2000, 2001 by Galway Kinnell. Reprinted by permission of Houghton Mifflin Harcourt Publishing Company and Carcanet Press Ltd. All rights reserved.

PHILIP LARKIN: 'Broadcast' and 'Talking in Bed' from *Collected Poems*, edited by Anthony Thwaite (Faber and Faber, 1988). Copyright © 1988, 1989 by the Estate of Philip Larkin. Reprinted by permission of the publisher.

TIM LIARDET: 'Needle on Zero' from *To the God of Rain* (Seren, 2003) reprinted by permission of the publisher.

LIZ LOCHHEAD: 'Morning After' from *Collected Poems* (Polygon, 1984), reprinted by permission of Polygon, an imprint of Birlinn Ltd (www.birlinn.co.uk).

LOUIS MACNEICE: 'Coda' and 'And love hung still as crystal over the bed' from *Collected Poems,* edited by E. R. Dodds (Faber and Faber, 2007). Copyright © the Estate of Louis MacNeice. Reprinted by permission of David Higham Associates Ltd.

OLIVIA MCCANNON: 'Timing' and 'Ironing', copyright © Olivia McCannon, 2009. Reprinted by permission of the author

PHYLLIS MCGINLEY: 'The 5:32' from *Times Three* (Secker & Warburg, 1961), reprinted by permission of The Random House Group Ltd and Pollinger Ltd.

ROGER MCGOUGH: extract from 'Summer with Monika' from *Summer with Monika* (Penguin, 1991), reprinted by permission of PFD (*www.pfd.co.uk*) on behalf of Roger McGough.

JAMES MERRILL: 'A Renewal' from *Collected Poems*, edited by J. D. McClatchy and Stephen Yenser, copyright © 2001 by the Literary Estate of James Merrill at Washington University. Reprinted by permission of Alfred A. Knopf, a division of Random House, Inc.

ANNE MICHAELS: 'Three Weeks' from *Skin Divers*. Copyright © Anne Michaels, 1999. Published in the UK by Bloomsbury Publishing PLC and in Canada by McClelland & Stewart Ltd. Reprinted by permission of the publishers.

EDNA ST VINCENT MILLAY: 'When I too long have looked upon your face' from *Collected Poems of Edna St Vincent Millay*, edited by Norma Millay (Harper & Row, 1956). Copyright © 1921, 1948, by Edna St. Vincent Millay. Reprinted by permission of Elizabeth Barnett, Literary Executor, The Millay Society.

ADRIAN MITCHELL: 'Celia Celia' from *Greatest Hits* (Bloodaxe Books, 1991). Copyright © Adrian Mitchell, 1991. Reprinted by permission of PFD (*www.pfd.co.uk*) on behalf of the Estate of Adrian Mitchell. Adrian Mitchell Educational Health Warning! None of Adrian Mitchell's poems to be used in connection with any examinations whatsoever!

JOHN MONTAGUE: 'All Legendary Obstacles' from *Collected Poems* (Gallery Press, 1995), reprinted by permission of the author and The Gallery Press, Loughcrew, Oldcastle, County Meath, Ireland.

EDWIN MORGAN: 'One Cigarette' and 'Strawberries' from *Collected Poems* (Carcanet, 1990). Copyright © Edwin Morgan, 1990. Reprinted by permission of the publisher.

OGDEN NASH: 'Reprise' first printed in the *New Yorker*, copyright © 1974 by Ogden Nash, renewed, reprinted by permission of Curtis Brown, Ltd.

354

355

Index of Poets

Index of Titles and First Lines

THE STORY OF PENGUIN CLASSICS

Before 1946 ... 'Classics' are mainly the domain of academics and students; readable editions for everyone else are almost unheard of. This all changes when a little-known classicist, E. V. Rieu, presents Penguin founder Allen Lane with the translation of Homer's *Odyssey* that he has been working on in his spare time.

1946 Penguin Classics debuts with *The Odyssey*, which promptly sells three million copies. Suddenly, classics are no longer for the privileged few.

1950s Rieu, now series editor, turns to professional writers for the best modern, readable translations, including Dorothy L. Sayers's *Inferno* and Robert Graves's unexpurgated *Twelve Caesars*.

1960s The Classics are given the distinctive black covers that have remained a constant throughout the life of the series. Rieu retires in 1964, hailing the Penguin Classics list as 'the greatest educative force of the twentieth century.'

1970s A new generation of translators swells the Penguin Classics ranks, introducing readers of English to classics of world literature from more than twenty languages. The list grows to encompass more history, philosophy, science, religion and politics.

1980s The Penguin American Library launches with titles such as *Uncle Tom's Cabin*, and joins forces with Penguin Classics to provide the most comprehensive library of world literature available from any paperback publisher.

1990s The launch of Penguin Audiobooks brings the classics to a listening audience for the first time, and in 1999 the worldwide launch of the Penguin Classics website extends their reach to the global online community.

The 21st Century Penguin Classics are completely redesigned for the first time in nearly twenty years. This world-famous series now consists of more than 1300 titles, making the widest range of the best books ever written available to millions – and constantly redefining what makes a 'classic'.

The Odyssey continues ...

The best books ever written

PENGUIN 🐧 CLASSICS

SINCE 1946

Find out more at www.penguinclassics.com